GOOD FOR ONE RIDE

GARY MCGINNIS

Good for One Ride

Copyright © 2013 by Gary McGinnis

ISBN-10: 1530481422
ISBN-13: 978-1530481422

Acclaim for Good for One Ride

I'm forty-five years from The Tet Offensive in Vietnam, but I remember it as if the bodies in the streets of Hue were still warm. I've read hundreds of books about that war and written several myself, but the one thing that most often eludes these stories, my own included, is the terrifying sense of anticipation that every soldier carries through every day and then brings home to live with for the rest of his life, should he be so lucky. To feel that every second in a war zone holds the origin of your oblivion and to realize once you leave that you are living on time borrowed from corpses is emotionally exhausting and almost impossible to put into words. And yet, Gary McGinnis has managed to do just that with grace and lyricism and great honesty. His book *Good for One Ride* is a small book in terms of pages, but it is a huge story. If you read it, you will understand the scourge of Post-Traumatic Stress Disorder that curses combat veterans forever. This is an important work and only enhances the Vietnam War literature that has come before.

—Jim McGarrah, author of *A Temporary Sort of Peace*, winner 2010 Eric Hoffer Award

This vivid short novel utterly transports the reader to the field of war: its infinite manifestations of fear and dreamlike connection and nightmarish loss. In each section the protagonist enters a more terrifying zone of psychological transformation. On every page, the skillful storytelling conveys the immediate effects and the permanent consequences of situations the narrator describes this way: "I strained to see enemy movements everywhere, to feel beyond my senses, to know without reason, to hear without hearing, to become united with the stench and to endure." Gary McGinnis has written a wise, haunting story that is a remarkable gift to our nation at this moment when our citizens wish to honor and to truly make the effort to understand the soldiers returning to us and those who cannot return.

—Kevin McIlvoy, author of *Little Peg*

To Anita

In Memory of:

Ed O'Connor, Marine, Vietnam

Born 12 November 1946

KIA 17 June 1966

* * * *

Jim Proulx, Vietnam Veteran

Born 18 September 1942

Died 23 March 1967

* * * *

Ken Laundry, Navy Pilot

Born 1 October 1943

Died 27 April 1983

Contents

Preface

Monsoon rain and wind whipped against my face and back as I crawled inside the generator trailer to sleep. I tied the canvas cover twine to the metal thongs on the outside of the trailer. It prevented the rain from blowing the flap open and drenching me during the night. I pushed the generator to one side and placed my air mattress on the floor in the open space. Lying beneath a light nylon poncho liner, my senses grasped the fleeting traces of the night. I smelled the new canvas cover, the gasoline and oil spilled, and the rope twine used to tie the canvas down. The smell of twine reminded me of the bales of hay I had slung in the Vermont summers of my youth. Gripping the twine that bound the hay, I tossed the bales into hot stale barns. Now I heard the wind sweep and the rain pelt against the sides of the trailer. I realized the total darkness of my cell and I felt the quiet awful nausea of knowing I had no purpose in this place. And here I'd sleep in proxy for my country's weak.

I dreamt of a woman standing alone beside Big Top Lake in Cold River, Vermont. I saw her face clearly, her friendly eyes and smile, the evidence of her tenacious quiet strength drawn firmly into place by her straight physique. The gentle waves at shore licked the hem of her clean white summer dress and spilled over her little feet, and then retraced. She picked up her wide brimmed hat and placed it upon her head so that the front brim tilted into Saturn's rings. Her eyes were sad distractions to my sleep. Beneath their quiet watch I heard from without a steady rising blast. A rocket closely launched high and roaring loudly aimed directly at our point. I stood to pry the wetted knots of twine but they would not give. The roar descended straight upon me. I could not move but listened for the rocket's final pound…

She Couldn't Wave Back

Homefires

Crooked pedals

Broken spokes

The road winding steep.

Carry the cold night air,

Dark and unfriendly,

To home fires,

The only warmth

That house could give.

Brisk attic interlude

Frosted windows

Buffalo robe

Ancient tears.

* * * *

Before daybreak, I dreamt of Vermont skies in summer. Dark twisters lifted the soil into the air. The skies turned into dark red ashes and soot.

Eagles spread the ashes over the entire country, as marching children in crisp, green uniforms passed before my father, saluting him. They had no faces. Their bayonets fixed, their weapons were shouldered through taunt canvas straps. Young eyes suddenly surfaced. They peered out from beneath heavy pot-helmets, as the little soldiers marched in dreary unison toward the shadow of dark green valleys.

Asleep, I merely dreamt but soon awoke in darkness to feel the familiar conscious dread. I arose from the sagging relic of a bed and twisted the light bulb in the naked ceiling fixture. The light flickered before it lit the room.

I dressed quietly.

I stood in the doorway and observed the room for one last time. I said goodbye to the gray pitched walls, the buffalo-robe bedspread, the compact television lying on a tall gun cabinet and the closet filled with my clothes from another lifetime. Closing the door, the sound of the latch echoed in the room behind me.

Downstairs, I felt the cold breeze in the hallway as it seeped through the cracks of the poorly insulated back door and the loosely fitted large window frame.

Looking through the window at the cold Vermont morning, the wind swept snow against the south wall of the farmhouse while the dry rafters creaked and groaned.

My father scowled as he gathered his implements for work. He wore a fresh, green outfit of work shirt and matching trousers. He had buffed his black steel-toed work shoes without polish, and he had tucked his safety glasses into his front pocket beside two tall yellow pencils. As he hastily drank coffee, he looked often at the clock. His favorite red and black checkered hunting coat lay folded in his lap.

My mother had draped her beige imitation fur coat and her black woolen kerchief across the back of one of the red vinyl kitchen chairs. A cigarette dangled from her mouth, and the smoke bothered her eyes, but she allowed it, as she paced about the kitchen, fussing over the housekeeping.

I stood in the kitchen in my Army dress uniform, looking across the tree line east of the flat meadow. Another snowy breath of winter rattled through the desolate trees, rooted upon the barren hillside. Their colorful leaves, not long departed, lay spent on frozen, rain-soaked soil. I saw deer, survivors of the November hunting season venture out safely, but with jitters, to their old haunts—wild crab apple trees in the tall brown grassy field.

My father said it was time to go, and he looked at me momentarily before he cast his eyes downward. My mother copied his stoic mood, but I felt anguish churning inside her like an uninvited spirit.

In a silence he dominated, my father drove us to his workplace, where men scurried into the shop, their lives evaporating into the air with each frosty breath steaming upward. I stood outside the car in anticipation, waiting for my father to speak.

"Learn about the war quickly," he said. "Get involved and understand it. Never take anything for granted. Write to your mother."

His eyes looked like serious globes, reflecting unfamiliar thoughts and emotions.

He shook my hand, walked up the concrete steps, never looking back, and then disappeared inside the General Electric plant.

My mother cried continuously while she drove to the

small airport one hour away.

She wailed terribly.

Finally, I told her, "Damn it, quit carrying on. How do you think it makes me feel? I got to go through this, and you're not helping me with all your bawling."

"I know, it must be awful for you, but I can't help it. It hurts too much."

She began to cry again, and before long she reached the same pitch and volume as before.

I saw her standing alone on the pavement in the miserably cold wind, huddled to herself, as she watched the small plane maneuver around. I waved to her from a window above the right wing, but I saw she couldn't wave back.

The Beginning of All Things

The veterans strenuously yelled

And applauded the new troops

Passing slowly before them

Beginners, replacements

Ripe for the harvest

Flesh for their leaders

Assigned for the year.

The veterans stood watching

With eyes made for staring

They stood cheering and jeering

Survivors at last.

They cheered for themselves

For having endured,

They yelled like old men

Suddenly pardoned,

Their youth sold away.

They waved enemy flags

Rifles, pistols and knives,

Shadows of sad wild men

Compressed into faded fatigues.

Their sun-bleached mustaches

Were long turned down at the corners,

Surely the Passover Angel stood near.

* * * *

The jet landed in Tan Son Nhut airport, where a senior staff sergeant, clipboard propped against his hip, led us inside a monstrous hangar—acres of concrete and metal. In the metal horizon, I barely heard an unfamiliar noise, and as we walked farther in, it became louder but still indistinguishable. Finally, I saw in the far distance an odd shape moving, contracting and expanding like a large amoeba. Closer, it sounded like the faint roar of a distant jet engine. Then I recognized the collective voice of men shouting, and as we drew near, I saw American soldiers waving their arms, their faces contorted, yelling, cheering and jeering, and I knew it was just for us. They held strange weapons, pistols and knives, flags from the enemy, tattered and worn. Their eyes were glazed and tormented. I knew we would end up like them if we lived through the year.

A sergeant yelled something, and the veterans grabbed their belongings and rushed toward the freedom plane that had brought us.

Outside the hangar, we loaded into buses with each window encased in metal mesh. Escorted by a three-quarter with a soldier manning a .50 caliber machine gun, we reached the Long Bien Reception Center. We filled out paperwork until nearly evening then ate donuts and drank orange juice in the mess hall. A lifer sergeant gave a little speech. He said the VC had rigged the latrines even there, and Americans had died.

Finally, a weary staff sergeant, Hess led me up a slight hill toward two isolated billets. He carried some of my lighter gear as we walked silently.

The sun sprayed faint red and orange light across freshly constructed unfinished buildings. I smelled the familiar scent of recent carpentry, of clean wood and sawdust, and I watched as the sun's rays cast an eerie shawl over the nearby sloping cradle of land.

The sergeant opened the door to a small billet.

"You'll stay here tonight. Alone. Mess is at 0600 and formation 0700. You'll be assigned work detail every day until they ship you out to your unit. Get some rest."

I removed a green camouflaged poncho liner from my duffel bag and spread it over a bunk next to an open screened window. I sat on the bunk and felt a slight breeze blow across my face as I watched the sun's final rays transform into shadows that spread like claws inside my stomach. Immediately, I heard the first of several distant explosions rip into my consciousness, and I couldn't tell if the explosions were outgoing or incoming. In the distance, several helicopters circled above the valley. Armed with miniguns, they began firing rounds, lighting the sky with tracers, spewing red dots down into a dark area beyond the cradle of land about a mile away.

I fell asleep, but it wasn't for long. Startled awake, I sat and looked out the window into the sky above the valley. It remained lit with flares and gunfire. Helicopters maneuvered in familiar circles, while American artillery continued to bear down on some gritty little fiend, armed for a cause unpopular to the United States government.

In the morning, the Army assigned us meaningless details. After mess I returned to my empty billet alone and watched it grow dark. Occasionally, artillery fired from the same position as the night before, but there were no helicopters circling and firing miniguns with red tracers. Flares did not rise in the distance, but artillery fired most of the night.

Late morning of the next day, we gathered in the ordnance building to receive our weapons. I felt anger and disbelief when I realized the weapons issued were not the standard M-14 with its familiar long wooden stock and barrel. Instead, they issued a smaller weapon, the M-16, built with a black plastic stock and grip. It looked too light and undependable, like a play-toy made by Mattel. It wasn't the weapon I had trained with in Fort Jackson, South Carolina, and with which I had fired expertly at the rifle range in basic training. I remembered sighting in the M-14 by creating three over-lapping bullet holes in a target at fifty meters: three clicks left to right and five clicks up for elevation to hit the bulls-eye. I had disassembled, cleaned, reassembled, fired at the shooting range, and lived with some comfort that I knew the weapon and the weapon knew me. What little security I felt was being taken away from me by a fat lifer with bulging purple veins covering his nose like a topographical map. I watched him as he toiled to copy serial numbers from a completely different weapon. All I could hear was his heavy breathing and perceive his sense of safety. His dangerous tour would require theft of steaks and whisky from officers' supply, and he'd spend late afternoon in a frigging hammock.

Then, as if on cue, he had the wisdom to recite a favorite Army slogan: "Move out, boy, Jody's home screwing your girlfriend."

Sergeant Hess stood nearby and saw my reaction. "What's the matter boy, you don't like the M-16?"

"I don't know anything about it, and it's a little late to get acquainted don't you think?"

"That's your problem, you think too much," he said. "The M-16's automatic. It's faster. In the Nam when it gets thick, it's not always long distance."

He mimicked my worried expression. "If you're not in the infantry you're not even here."

Then he yelled at us to fall out in the yard for formation. Minutes later we lined up outside and about twenty-five of us loaded into two deuce-and-a-halves, led by a three-quarter, manned with a .50 caliber machine gun. The trucks stopped at the entrance to a bare open field shaped in a rectangular five acres or so, surrounded by thick jungle. The length of the field sloped downward for about one-eighth of a mile, and on the opposite side from the entrance, a partially bordered small marsh extended into more jungle.

We gathered around Hess who pointed to the field, sighed, and said, "Observe the foxholes you will occupy tonight by threes. You will pull guard duty two hour shifts per individual. This is not a drill. Some of you will be assigned starlight scopes. Lose one and you will be court martialed. Move out."

I reached mid-field and inspected the foxholes that were wide shallow and smooth. I decided the middle section would be the most defendable if we were attacked, and the enemy would have to go through a few people before it got to me. As I wondered why the shallow fox holes were so smooth, I noticed two soldiers watching me select the position, and seemed to discuss if they should join me. The first man to arrive was short, extremely emaciated, heavily tattooed and soaked in sweat. His red headed partner, who was tall and powerfully built, soon followed.

Red asked, "What do you make of all this?"

"Lot of GIs before us had used this field," I finally replied.

I looked at the strange thin guy and noticed the entire circumference of his spindly arms displayed permanent ink drawings of little imagination. What appeared to be blue and red spider webs spanned down his forearms into his fingers. Traces of web highlighted his throat.

"I'll take the first shift," I told them.

Red took the second and the thin man had no choice.

"Who you with?" Red asked.

"Combat Engineers."

"You going to build us roads?" he asked sarcastically.

I didn't answer him.

"We're cooks. What the hell do they expect from us?"

He swept his hands through his thick hair and then lit a cigarette.

"Cooks can die too, you know," I said.

"You got it all figured out, huh? Been here before?"

"Find your own foxhole. I don't need you fuckers here."

Red and I stared at each other briefly.

He said unconvincingly, "No offense. I'm a little tense, that's all."

"We both are," the thin man said. "Let's just hang together tonight."

He studied me with eerie passive eyes, and then he got up and took off his fatigue shirt, displaying tattoos that covered his entire body from his neck to his waist.

I recoiled noticeably.

"Do my tattoos bother you?" he asked in a sultry voice.

"Why did you do all that?" I asked.

"I grew up in New York City down the street from a tattoo parlor. The old man liked me a lot and he offered to give me tattoos if I did him favors. So I got this one right here on my chest." It looked like several demons and two toll booths surrounded by a faded red heart.

"It's my mother's heart," he said.

Red laughed.

"What's that supposed to mean?" I asked, and then wondered what kind of favors he did for the old man.

"What's your problem?" Hess asked me as he suddenly stood beside our foxhole.

"There's nothing wrong, Sergeant," Red replied. "It's just that this man here made us all laugh. He's a funny guy."

I gathered my gear and stood beside Hess.

"I'm not staying with them."

Hess chuckled. "Come with me, Garrett."

I followed him a few yards to another foxhole occupied by an Italian-American sergeant. Hess left as it grew dark and the Italian handed me a starlight scope while I took the first watch. The scope was engineered to reflect the celestial lights, but the night offered nothing and I saw only vague green images swirling into shapes resembling ghosts or dancing trees. Nothing stood still.

Later Hess returned, laughing to himself in a kind of quiet choking manner, and then he tugged the Italian's pant leg.

"I had to save this poor bastard. He had those two screw-ups with him. Both of them!"

His body shook. When he calmed down some, he said, "Sergeant Wills is staying with them now."

I picked up the starlight scope again while a pack of light colored flying insects hovered above my face, drifting in and out of my vision, and they moved in formation like a restless ball, like new recruits struggling to make sense of their feelings. For whatever reason nature instructed the flying creatures to appear, they disappeared as mysteriously.

The Italian grunted. "My watch now."

I removed my poncho from my ammo belt, draping it over the smoothest portion of the foxhole, resting my head on my left bicep and drifting off for about an hour. I awoke to the thin man's cries nearby.

"Sergeant! Sergeant! Wake up. I see something out

there."

"There's nothing out there," hollered Sergeant Wills, "You're looking at the jungle, numb nuts! What time is it?"

 Neither cook answered. I heard the sound of a kick and a moan and then the sergeant's angry voice, "I said what time is it!"

"I don't know," the thin man answered.

"You little cobweb son-of-a-bitch, don't wake me up again"

At daylight, Hess and the Italian assembled all of us and Hess said, "We are going to run through a little exercise. Follow the path through the brush and one of us will be right behind you." He stopped and looked at Red arranging Spiderman's rolled up poncho attached to his ammo belt.

"Get your shit together or you'll be back every night this month."

"Yes Sergeant," they responded in unison.

Hess continued, "On this path cardboard targets of VC will pop up. Identify and shoot them. Put your weapons on automatic and listen to our instructions as you proceed, and do exactly what we tell you."

He ordered a private to move out, followed by a sergeant, and when automatic fire erupted out of sight in the thickets, he ordered another man to run the course.

My turn came and the Italian sergeant followed me. We entered a winding path leading into a thicket and eventually a clearing, surrounded by huge trees and tall clumps of grass. I sprayed two stationary targets, peppering shrubbery and grass. Farther in, another target of a VC popped up and I fired two rounds into its "chest." A few more steps and two more targets popped up, one on both sides of the path. I fired into them. Three more targets appeared and I responded. In my periphery I spotted a sniper target camouflaged high in a tree. I fired one round.

"You saw him too late. You're dead," the Italian said.

After everybody finished the exercise, Hess loaded us into trucks and he said to me, "Get in, killer."

Yen and Xinh

We stood nervously waiting in the sun to hear our names called for unit assignments while the dust rose in the reception yard of the Long Bien pen. Some smoked cigarettes, inhaling the smoke too often, as they shuffled in place in the dust like barnyard beasts ready for shipment.

A staff sergeant read the unit assignments and I hoped beyond reason I would get a safe assignment. He blatted over the loudspeaker: "Private Theo Garrett, 2nd Infantry Division, 2nd Engineers."

Soon, I left Long Bien in a convoy with ten men in the back of a deuce-and-a-half. The troop carrier shook on the rough road, occasionally swerving to avoid civilian traffic. I watched the terrain, looking for the unknown and I blended into the harsh rhythm of the ride.

The thickets along the sides of the road were heavily coated with dust plastered from countless vehicles. The road smelled heavily of diesel fuel. Farther along, the convoy traveled on paved road behind a Vietnamese bus, over-loaded with civilians, crowding a narrow strip ahead. Some of the Vietnamese were clinging to the sides of the bus. Others, scattered along the roof, were clutching concealed leverages between great bundles of clothes, furniture and bicycles with their own versions of crooked pedals.

The convoy slowed to a crawl as it passed several small clusters of straw-thatched hooches. Outside, squatting Vietnamese gawked. Old Vietnamese women spat red betel nut juice, their teeth "attractive" red and their deep-water eyes smiling like cunning Buddhas. Perhaps they contemplated and prayed this to be their last life cycle: "*Please, no more wheel of the oxcart, no more rebirth, no more squatting.*" Their spirit-faces hidden deep within the squalor of their strange primitive world, they picked lice from one another's scalps, their voices cackled in unison, a talk-talk chant sounding like horses hooves galloping.

The truck moved forward and rumbled past more Vietnamese, selling something, wanting something. The blast of air from a speeding truck ahead of us blew a coolie hat off the head of one smiling Vietnamese woman. Everything seemed funny to them, but inside some of those laughing hosts bitter ideologies of war would spring. There existed no traces of it that day in the parched daylight, along the dry road that lead to the beginning of all things.

The convoy wheeled into Chung Quyen, a small town with a circular park at its entrance. Our truck rumbled along a dirt road past a two-storied hotel, then across a stagnant pond and into a small American base about seven hundred feet away. The shallow pond stretched about five hundred feet along the edge of the base facing the town and then it curved at a ninety degree angle away from the town. At that corner, a sandbagged bunker existed about five feet from the water and close to a water-point shack. Coils of concertina wire spread about thirty feet in rows into the pond and it formed a fan shape around the bunker and that corner of the base.

The truck stopped at a guard shack near the entrance and then drove straight to the water point where two water purification trucks operated. Both units were shut down. A chopper flew overhead and descended toward a landing pad about twenty feet from the motor pool and the water point. Three Vietnamese hooches were erected away from the base and the pad, separated by a small section of water.

The truck moved past the water point and stopped in

front of headquarters.

"This is where you get off, Garrett," a soldier in the cab shouted. "Your people are around here somewhere."

"You Private Theo Garrett?" a booming voice asked.

"Yes," I replied, jumping off the truck and looking at a huge man standing before me.

"I'm your platoon sergeant, Monroe Balsam." He shook hands with me; his grasp too light. "I bet you wonder why you not in Bearcat."

"I don't know where the hell I am."

Balsam laughed. "Here's not so bad, but in Bearcat they army you to death. Most the time that's where I have to be. I go back there in a few days after I get you settled, and you be here for the time being. Spec 4 Bates, he in charge." Balsam chuckled to himself.

I didn't know what to say, so I looked at the ground and noticed his polished boots and clean starched fatigues.

"Your paperwork say you went to college. Is that true?"

"I went to junior college for a couple years."

Balsam lazily scratched his big forehead. "You the only man in our platoon who been to college. Mister, you had to do something right to get that far."

"Well it wasn't far enough."

Balsam laughed again and then spit on the ground. He began to walk along in a contrived cool stride. There was a hitch in his walk as if he were made differently from other men. Perhaps a joint or something flared out within his anatomy that caused him to strut-bop occasionally. For some reason it didn't occur on every step and only on the left side of his body.

He stopped in the middle of a boardwalk, allowing two middle-aged sergeants to pass. "Maybe you can help me when the Colonel wants me to write reports?"

"Sure."

"The old man wants to know everything we do. He make us platoon sergeants write reports he call "*bullets*." Don't he know we see enough real bullets?" He paused. "Man, you sure be helping me out."

He kept moving slowly again, and I followed him.

"The smart-ass lieutenants make fun of what I write."

"I'm not great at it, but I can help you, Sarge."

We didn't talk the rest of the way to the water shack, but Balsam whistled, undoubtedly thrilled with his new literary acquisition.

"This is it."

Inside the shack he showed me an empty top bunk.

"You the fourth guy from our platoon in here, and then there's one transit who stay over there." He pointed to a bunk by itself against the wall. "Get yourself situated. I need to see someone in headquarters but I be back in a while."

"I'm not going anywhere."

Balsam smiled and left the shack.

I put my gear inside an empty green wall locker, then sat in a chair and looked around. The shack was built with scraps of lumber and large strips of metal that had been hammered into portions along all of the walls. Two doors hung crudely. Gaping cracks existed at the top of the door that led to the only bunker outside, facing the town. Dirt smothered the uneven floor, boarded carelessly, cropping up fortunately in places where it appeared the least traffic flowed. In the middle of the windowless room, a hand-made table stored bread, butter, paper and clutter. Two double bunks and three single bunks took up most of the space. Metal rod frames rose approximately four feet above each single bunk securing thin green nylon mosquito nets that were rolled up and tied. I became aware of a pecking order. A filthy white parachute billowed in spots where it had been nailed to the ceiling. Another poorly hung door faced the motor pool.

* * * *

Balsam had returned to Bearcat, leaving Spec 4 Bates in charge of the water point. Two of the watermen were not back from Bearcat yet, and the transit kept dramatically to himself. He chained and locked his trunk of belongings before leaving the shack, and his energy followed him like a shadow—and some of it guarded his space when he left. He never spoke to anyone. He had scribbled with a magic marker on his trunk, great and terrible threats, promising to kill anyone stupid enough to touch his stuff. I didn't know what the man did in the Army, and I didn't really want to know.

I concentrated on learning the purification system, the erdulator: how to create a flock and keep it together to draw dirt out of the water, how to run the slurries, use the right chemicals, backwash and distribute the clean water into clean tanks, and miscellaneous chores that became routine by the middle of January.

By then heavy rains had mixed with the dry dust to form mud that covered the motor pool about two feet in most places. Engineering had laid down large strips of heavy metal fastened together by tongue and groove. The metal web allowed huge equipment unrestricted passage throughout the motor-pool.

Bates and I were standing in the yard when two GIs drove up to the shack in a three-quarter, and the driver got out first.

"The big guy's Paul Smith," Bates said. "And the other character is Jeffrey Wright. They're both from our platoon. They're coming back from Bearcat."

"Bitch," Jeffrey Wright said as he got out of the truck on the passenger's side. Mud crept up his leg, soiling his tapered fatigue pants. Moisture oozed over his boot tops. The sun hadn't shined for several days, but Wright wore sunglasses. He was a scrawny man built like a bowling pin, and he grunted as he pulled his bag from the truck. The bag opened. Letters and his shaving kit fell into the mud. He swore again, his anger lacking gravity.

Bates held his stomach and wrenched around as though he were in pain. I grinned.

"Listen to that fool. I'd hate to hear him if something serious happened to him," Bates said.

"Need some help?" I offered.

"Yeah, guess I do."

I helped him pick up his letters.

"Hey, you're the new guy," he said. "I'm Jeffrey Wright and this here's Paul Smith."

Wright shook my hand vigorously while Smith moved closer to get a better look at me and then shook my hand. Bates moved next to Jeffrey and put his hand on his shoulder. "Did you see Raquel Welch?"

"Did I ever. Right up close."

"You weren't as close as me. I was up real close," Smith

said. "Not Wright. I told him to go early, but no, he knows everything."

Wright playfully elbowed Bates in the ribs.

"You should have heard old Smith. His bunk never stopped squeaking all night."

"She was real pretty," Smith said. "Sure were a lot of guys there in Bearcat. It didn't seem much like Christmas though."

Bates ran his hand through his hair. "I'm sure everybody was thinking about Christ when they saw her ass."

"She had a good one," Smith replied dreamily.

Wright's laugh sounded like worn out bearings in a water pump. Smith grinned at me. "He's got a funny laugh, huh?"

We went inside and sat at the table.

"You just get assigned here?" Wright asked.

"Can't you tell by my new baggy pants?"

"Well, you can take them to the tailor in town," Smith advised. "He'll fix them up for you real cheap. Make them fit perfect. It'll make you feel better. I know."

"Where do I go?"

"There's another small firebase," Wright said. "On the other side of town where we pick up the mail and parts for the erdulator. There's a big helicopter pad at that firebase."

Wright stared at Smith.

"Down the street a ways from there, there's a whorehouse. I keep trying to get Smith interested in going but he's chicken."

Smith looked down at the table and studied his dirty fingernails.

"Next to the whorehouse is the tailor," Wright added.

"You can go into the whorehouse and leave your pants with the tailor," Smith said. "When you get through with the ladies, you can wear your new pants."

"Ladies?" Wright asked. His angry face transformed quickly into a smile for me. His smile displayed big yellow teeth.

"What do you know about the whores over there anyway?" he asked. "You never been with a whore."

Aside to me, Wright added, "He's from Idaho."

"Well, I've had whores before," Smith said.

"When did you ever have one? Huh? Tell me, you liar."

Paul Smith slumped in his chair. His thin blond hair fell across his eyes. He swept the hair back and then sat up. He looked strong enough to kill Wright with a mild slap. His huge shoulders were drawn forward toward his barrel chest.

"I've had girls in the circus," Smith said. "They stopped in my hometown once. And I saw all the shows. I was asked to go back in the tent where they slept. That's where I had one."

Bates chuckled while making eye contact with me.

"You're so full of it, Smith. It's a wonder you can even see straight. This hillbilly is afraid to go with me on the mail runs because I always stop at the whorehouse."

"Well, those women get sick. I don't want to get sick," Smith said.

Waving his arms above his head, Wright shouted,

"You never been laid so quit acting like you know anything about it."

"The next time you go there, I'll show you who's afraid of them," yelled Smith, his face turning red.

Wright's mouth gaped open, his face twisted with delight. "Did you guys hear what he just said?"

"Give it a rest, Wright," Bates ordered. "If he doesn't want to get laid, that's his business."

Wright stared at Smith. "The next time we go on the mail run, that's it for you, circus boy!"

In the background, a chopper landed at the pad, its blades whipping the air.

"So, did you like Raquel Welch?" I asked Smith.

Smith grinned widely and shook his head in amazement.

"I was right up close to the stage when she came out. She wore a white fur bikini. She danced and sang, and I just wanted to squeeze her."

Smith buried his face in his elbow, shook his head and made gurgling sounds. He lifted his head. "She even had this one GI come up on the stage with her, and he just goes right up to her and grabs her left boob. I couldn't believe it. She just took him by the wrist and pulled his hand away and kept right on dancing like it never happened."

Bates stirred like he remembered something irritating and his voice grew harsh. "You need to pay attention out there, Wright. Balsam says the water doesn't taste good when you work it. Show me what the hell you're doing."

Bates and Wright left the hooch. Smith followed.

I went outside and sat on a row of sandbags near the bunker next to the water. A light drizzle of rain picked up and sunlight filtered through dark clouds spreading rays across the pond's surface water. Shocks of rainbow colors floated on the water's surface of discarded motor pool oil and gasoline.

Two youngsters, a boy about seven years old and his sister about five waved at me from shallow water approximately fifty feet left of the bunker.

The boy called out, "Shoeshine, shoeshine GI?" His thin legs poked through oversized blue gym shorts.

I had seen the children play together early evenings in

front of their little hooch while their parents watched. The little girl always wore only a pair of white underwear. She didn't have to do much to convince the world she was a beautiful child. She'd throw grass at her older brother who ran giggling and taunting her, and she never tired of chasing him. Her laughter and her footsteps echoed in her belly.

In the water, the youngsters drew closer to the bunker. I noticed the little girl's straight black bangs and her hair sculptured around her neck. Her slightly plump face smiled in anticipation as she hung on to her reliable brother who carried her wrapped around his belly when he maneuvered the wire. Her legs squeezed tightly together around his slender back.

They traversed through the large rolls of concertina wire as the barbs occasionally nipped the back of the boy's wrinkled, white short-sleeved shirt. She held a shoeshine kit strapped around her arm, as her brother controlled the wire above with his hands, and with his bare feet, he stood between the barbs on the wire below. When they reached me, the little boy began to clean my boots. The little girl stood a few feet away, blushing, her fingers in her mouth.

"What's your name?" I asked the boy.

"Yen."

"What's her name?"

"Xinh."

"She's very shy."

Yen turned to his sister and spoke rapidly.

I threw a pebble at her feet, and she giggled. She drew closer, and I talked to her and made faces and she giggled more. Occasionally, Yen stopped working to look at his sister. Yen had a narrow intelligent face. His eyes were set closely together.

Before long, Xinh sat in my lap and she rested her head on my chest, and I rocked her gently as a light drizzle faded. A pleasant breeze picked up, and Xinh closed her eyes, her right hand cupped near her mouth, her left arm draped around my chest and side.

Several minutes later, Yen said, "Okay GI all done."

I continued to rock the little girl in my arms and to Yen I rubbed the palm of my hands quickly back and forth.

"You do laundry?"

"Yes. Yes."

I pointed toward the shack. "More GIs in there."

Yen nodded.

I paid Yen, and he helped me count.

Xinh didn't move as Yen spoke angrily to her. She smiled at me and slowly lifted her head off my chest and she squeezed my hand.

Yen hissed at her again, and then he wrapped her around him. She smiled at me again just before she rode the wire.

Black Bangs

God and war were at opposite poles like pleasure and torture, like prostitutes and the Virgin Mary. Now, they have become one. It happened with a flash of light I saw. A sniper's round missed my face and dug into the bunker wall. I felt dread tear my heart with cold scissors. Will it ever mend this unapparent wound? Perhaps it keeps tearing as I go along. Finally, the heart falls from its place and takes a turn down inside my right leg or my left. The skin at the anklebone is strung so tightly there. The blood bursts forth. It fills my boot and sloshes around with every step. I hear it in my sleep and there is no resting place.

* * * *

Soft rain fell on the water shack while the men slept in the early morning of 10 February 1968. The smell of musty fatigues, collected to be washed, thrown into heaps about the shack, added to the stifling odor within. All dust had turned into monsoon mud everywhere outside and was carried in with soldiers' boots. The mud-caked room in which the soldiers slept was far better than sleeping in the rain like some. Dry bunks were partners there and blessings too, still loneliness slept lightly next to dread.

A thud, muffled and obscured, came from somewhere within the motor pool. I wrenched myself awake. Alert and moving, I yelled: "Incoming! Incoming!"

Quickly dressed, I collected my weapon and gear and on the way out the door shook Smith. I raced to the bunker alone. Minutes passed and still no one came outside the shack. Mortars continued to hit the base. I noticed my boots, laced to the top eyelets and tied, were on the wrong feet.

The night sky filled with American flares popped from flare guns. The floating lights suspended by tiny parachutes were set aloft in the airy breeze. A mortar pounded into the road next to the shack. The metal track laid just beneath the mud rose out of the earth, twisting in a sharp burst of heat. By then the men had finally fled the water shack and filled the bunker.

"Where's it coming from?" Smith asked.

"From the south side," I answered.

Just then multiple small arms fired from the outlying engagement, south. Fires erupted in several buildings. Flames and smoke consumed the white light offered by the southern flares. I could hear men yelling curses and see their silhouettes fighting the fires. Mortars pounded. AK-47s sprayed the southern front. M-16s responded.

I heard a frazzled Wright shout, "Will this bunker hold up?"

"They won't get us if nothing lands in the doorway," Smith hollered.

I saw more fire sweep into the sky along the southern border. Shocks of flame and crackling cinders sent sparks airborne, but a tall jet of water shot into the flames. The fire appeared weakened and the active silhouettes cast by the flames and the flares diminished. Small arms popped sporadically. Mortars no longer landed. I heard a rocket descend into the resistance there and felt a shiver pass through me.

Soldiers dragged three fresh bodies of American deceased across the muddy road near the water point and tucked them beside short sandbag walls, recently built by South Vietnamese civilians.

Then, creeping into earshot, the familiar rotary blade, slicing, thumping the air into hydraulic lift, it appeared. The entire left side of a chopper paused in full view before an opening in the west side of the bunker. Hovering above, it stopped in flight about ten feet above the water, its blade whipping tight shattering waves across the pond, the large rolls of concertina wire were blasted into retreat. The chopper maneuvered in the air ever so slightly. Its rear blade steadying the craft into position, then a blast of light, incomprehensible, so quick and deadly aimed, a rocket launched from its left side sailed directly into the straw hooch of Yen, Xinh with mom and dad. No more black bangs. No more play time. The hooch exploded into flames. No human stirred from within or without that blaze. The home melted into human allied chaff consumed by *friendly fire*. Then the looming craft turned its spotlight on the smoldering remains before it turned and flew away.

Smith said, "Maybe they got out."

"They didn't," I replied.

I heard American voices strained and distant, shouting. We listened and waited inside the bunker, occasionally hearing a sizzle and a pop as a flare lit the north side of the base closest to us. We waited a long time and nothing happened. We grew bored.

"Well, I guess it's over. I'm going inside the shack," Wright said.

Smith and I followed him outside the bunker. Wright went inside the shack while we waited outside for daylight.

Smith laughed when he saw my boots. "I won't tell anybody."

Soldiers carried the three American bodies and laid them next to the helicopter pad and placed them carefully on the ground, wrapping them in blankets, their boots poked out from beneath green woolen blankets.

"They won't be drinking our water anymore," Smith said.

I looked at Smith and wondered why he had said that.

"Well, there ain't nothing worth saying anyway, might as well make the best of it," he added, crossing his bulky arms. "I just wish we could do our jobs and not have to get shot at. This is just a little base. Why do they want to fight here?"

About an hour passed.

Wright came around the corner of the water shack dressed in clean fatigues and fresh boots, a green army blanket wrapped around his oddly built body.

"War over yet?" he asked.

Then he laughed self-consciously, his voice rasping. He stopped when he saw the three dead Americans, then he pulled the blanket around him more snugly. He sat down next to Smith and me on a bench along the west wall of the shack.

Smith turned to Wright. "I wonder if we're going to have breakfast this morning. That fire could have burnt down the mess hall."

"That's what we got c-rations for. For times like this. You'd only eat the cookies anyway," Wright chided.

"They never have enough cookies," Smith said sadly.

Wright laughed sadistically. His face, severely pockmarked, his huge forehead ballooned beneath an overgrown crew cut. The shape of his head looked like a slightly rounded wedge and it didn't match his skinny body. He had bloused his fatigue pants above his boots and they rode up his scrawny white legs.

He slurred most of his words but he could be

understood if you really paid attention. It were as though he practiced talking that way in the mirror.

Pulling the woolen army blanket from around his upper torso, he began to laugh in his familiar blatting style. He pointed at Smith. "This is Paul Smith."

He then lay upon his back on the ground, extending the blanket down to his ankles, leaving his boots sticking out and then he covered the rest of his body including his face. The outline of his breath pushed the blanket up and down above his mouth, his nose protruding, his voice speaking through the blanket of the playful dead. "This is Paul Smith."

Smith began to fidget. He nodded his giant head forward and tilted it to one side. "You shouldn't say things like that. I'd never do that to you."

Wright jumped up quickly, pulling the blanket away from him and holding it in one hand. Laughing, tears filled his eyes.

"Oh hell, I didn't mean nothing by it. We were just having a little fun, that's all."

He put his arm around Smith's shoulders and hugged him.

Smith remained staring at the ground, dashing his boot against small clods of mud, seeming to relish the attention.

"Come on, I was just kidding around," Wright continued.

Slowly, Smith lifted his face and smiled.

"Okay, but don't ever fool around like that again. It ain't funny if it's you who's dead."

Wright said sorrowfully, "It'll never happen again. I promise." Then he lay down again and covered himself the same way with the blanket. "This is Paul Smith," he said.

A colonel appeared. He looked weary and disturbed and spoke softly. "Is he the only casualty?" he asked pointing at Wright's still body under the blanket.

"Yes sir," I answered, hoping Wright could hold his breath.

The colonel paused for some time and then added, "A sergeant will come by later to identify the soldier. Gather his belongings and take his body to the pad."

"Yes sir."

With that he left.

Wright kept still.

I winked at Smith and said out loud, "Well sir, we think he's dead, he got hit by a mortar and he stopped breathing, I think, but we're not real sure. Maybe you should take a look at him."

Smith yanked the blanket off Wright.

"You bastards!" he hollered. "You want me to have a heart attack?" He crawled up to his knees. "I thought I was a goner for sure. Oh man."

"I'm hungry," said Smith. "I'm going over to see if they burned down the mess hall."

Wright went inside the shack.

I watched two soldiers load the three American bodies into a helicopter and I slung my weapon over my shoulder, tied the bandolier around my waist, took off my helmet and wiped the sweat from my brow. I walked to the mess hall and stood in line with other young men. Smoldering burnt rubble remained from the three buildings torched by enemy rockets.

After chow, Smith and I walked with some of the

infantry beyond the southern perimeter into the tall grass. There, mangled in the field, lay VC bodies ripped open by .50 caliber rounds. The thick black hair of one VC had been recently trimmed.

"I've seen enough," I said and began to leave.

"Wait for me," Smith said. "Wish we weren't here. I guess we have to stay awake all the time."

"You can try to save your life, but you don't own it. You do own the fear of losing it though," I said quietly.

"What?"

"Nothing."

We walked back to the water point, and Smith started the generator that supplied one truck with power, and I started the other one. About an hour later, trucks carrying empty water trailers pulled into the yard and waited in line for pure drinking water. We worked all day and into the night, purifying enough water in preparation for the early morning traffic.

The watermen slept that night in their fatigues and boots, their weapons and gear arranged for easy access. Earlier, Smith and Wright had moved the table out of the line of exit in case of another stampede. I got silly watching Wright's awkward movements. Smith had removed the clutter that had fallen on the floor from the table: spoons, plastic dishes, magazines and gloves, etc. He had swept the shack free of all the dried clods of mud. The dust had not settled fully as we began to sleep into the second night of our Tet Offensive.

At approximately 0200 hours a flare popped in the air above the pond. The watermen filled the bunker. The flares continued to light up the pond, the roadway leading into the town and the southern face of the hotel.

I looked at the hotel from one opening in the bunker, then bobbed to the next opening and looked quickly again before moving back to another position. I did this several times. Wright laughed. "Whatever you're trying to do, Garrett. It looks pretty silly."

I stopped, and could feel my heart beating.

The night became quiet except for the pop of flares. Occasionally, darkness enveloped the inside of the bunker—flares burning out, their small parachutes descending toward the water. Other flares soared quickly into the sky with a rushing sound similar to fireworks first launched. The new light traced the remains of the other burnt out flares. Small parachutes rocked in the breeze, casting shadows drifting across the inner bunker walls and descending diagonally across our faces.

I watched for movement toward the town outside the perimeter of the night-lights. The area was lit almost entirely, then, as though there existed an element of spectacle perceived by the soldiers in the base camp, Americans lined up, standing quietly at the edge of the pond facing the hotel.

They stood in the open, entirely without cover, forming one long line from the watermen's bunker to the roadway and the guard shack.

Bates went outside first. Then slowly Smith and Wright left the bunker and stood with the other men. I stayed inside.

"What are you doing in there? Everybody's out here," Smith said.

Something about it didn't feel right. I held my weapon tucked under my right arm as I crouched beneath the opening in the bunker wall facing the hotel.

"What are you doing in there?" Smith said again. "We're all out here."

Slowly I emerged and stood next to Smith. No one spoke. A splash of water sounded where a sinking tiny parachute and burnt flare landed.

I stood facing the hotel, eyeing the windows along the second story. The flares continued to breathe lightly, waving and dropping gently until they died. Darkness. A white flash erupted from the hotel window in the second story, directly in line with my vision. Another flare lit up the window, and I saw the dark figure of a man run past the window next to the flash and disappear into the darkness. I felt a rip in my heart. I turned and looked at the sandbag in the bunker next to my face and saw sand trickling down from the bullet hole. I stirred the hole with my finger and then touched Smith's shoulder.

"A sniper just shot at me," I said and showed Smith the hole in the sandbag and pointed toward the window in the hotel. "I saw the guy running in there."

A captain walked up to us. "Was there a shot fired at this position?"

"I saw a flash from that hotel window, but I didn't hear the shot," I replied. My voice felt like it didn't belong to me, like it was coming from someone else. I showed the captain the hole in the bunker sandbag and said, "It was meant for me."

"I saw the flash," the captain said. He looked at me. "God must have a plan for your life."

Top

Two weeks passed routinely after the attacks. We re-established an effective, orderly work schedule, but stress manifested itself in different ways. Wright's mispronounced monologues with intervals of blatting laughter leveled off into clearer sentences. He demanded more of himself at work, closely following the water purification procedures Bates had demanded. After work and during the night hours, he began reading western novels. He cleaned his weapon and his quarters and stopped picking on Smith.

Bates walked and moved more slowly. He was extremely quiet and didn't eat much. In the evenings he wrote letters to his girlfriend, but he never smiled while writing them.

As the days passed, I felt myself taking rapid shallow breaths and I sighed often. My hands occasionally trembled while using tools, but the tremors were hardly noticeable by the others.

Lastly, Smith lived in a mood of penance. He told me that he had made a pact with God after receiving a religious medal in the mail from his mother. The cross bore a hooded top on the vertical bar and a massive chain looped through the hood. Its godly length was long enough in circumference for the necks of two devoted soldiers, so he tied it into a knot that rested in the hollow of his Adam's apple.

He took the medal from around his neck one late afternoon and showed it to me at the table. "I'm a Catholic," he said. "Do you like it?"

"Never saw one any nicer."

Smith smiled proudly and practically blushed. Adjusting himself, he squirmed in his wooden chair. "Do you belong to a church?"

"No. But I feel like there's a connection between me and God, but it's contradictory."

"Why?"

"It's a mystery," I replied, smiling to myself. "When I was eleven, I went to Bible camp in the summer. Schroon Lake in New York State. A friend went with me, and I got religion, but I could sense it leaving me right after I got home after a couple weeks. Strange thing to sense for a kid. My friend became a Marine right after high school graduation. June 17, 1964. He got killed over here exactly two years later to the day.

He was a better man than me."

Paul shrugged his massive shoulders. "Do you think God will protect us if we stay close to Him?"

"He'll help you get through it, whatever that is, but there's no guarantee. Even if God talked to you out loud, you could still get blown away." I saw Smith frown, so I added, "I know he'd treat you different than me because he knows I don't like Him."

"You don't like Him?"

"Nah."

"He knows I like Him!" Smith said.

The shack door opened to a cool night breeze and a hillbilly-looking sergeant entered. He carried a duffle bag, weapon and ammo, helmet and flak vest. The sergeant dropped his muddy gear on the empty bunk next to the north wall where the angry man had slept before moving on to another assignment.

"I'm John Everett."

I introduced myself and Smith.

"I need to stay here for a few days before I head south," Everett said. "I sure could use a shower. I used to work in Water Supply. Damn sure did. You can't get any rank in Water though."

"Do you remember how to get everything running?" I asked.

"Yeah, it wasn't so long ago. I think I can do it." He pulled from his duffle bag a partial quart of whiskey. "You guys want some of this?"

I took a canteen cup from my wall locker while Smith scowled at me. "You better not drink that," Smith said.

Everett chuckled as he poured me a full cup.

"I take it he don't like whiskey.

"He's all right. Listen, I'll help you get the equipment running." I pointed in the direction of the trucks, south of the shack. "Bring your shower stuff out there when you're ready."

"I appreciate it."

"Thanks for the drink."

"There's more where that came from."

I went outside and turned on the generator and got the water running, and later Everett took his shower.

After I shut down the unit, I sat with him outside next to the shack, drinking whiskey.

"You know, Garrett, you're not like most guys in the Army your age. They're uptight. You know. They think they have power when they don't. But you don't act that way. I've been in the Army seventeen years, and I like it. But I did that time when things were different. The new guys coming in now are nothing like the old school. You know what I mean?"

He poured the last of the whiskey into my cup.

"I haven't thought about it. I don't belong in the Army."

Everett jumped up. "I'm going to get some beer. You want to come?"

"No."

He laughed and slapped me on the back. "You're going to help me drink it, right?"

"Where you getting it from?" I slurred.

"I know some people around here."

"I hate to tell you this, Everett, but I'm seeing double."

"Sit back and relax, I'll be back in a minute."

Everett walked around the corner of the shack, and I lay on my back on the bench and looked up into the night sky.

"You all right, Garrett?" Smith's voice blended into the sky.

"I'm all right."

"Why don't you come inside and go to sleep."

I giggled. "Ah, I feel like being out here and getting wasted. Haven't you ever felt that way?"

"Where's that sergeant?"

"He went to find the old school and get some beer."

I placed my left hand, palm up, across my forehead still lying on the bench.

"I'm going back inside," Smith said.

"Okay buddy."

I fell asleep. About an hour had passed when Everett shook me.

"Wake up, Private. We got some serious drinking to

do. Come on, get up."

I sat up and Everett handed me a beer.

"Come here soldier. Looky here. See what I got," Everett said.

"What is it, Looky Here?" I asked and then laughed.

"I got the Company Commander's jeep, and I know where there's a whorehouse in town. I mean a damn good one. French Vietnamese women. Oooh la la."

"I'm happy for you," I said.

"Well, you're coming too, bub. You're riding shotgun."

I drank some beer and looked across the water where the children had played. Nausea filled my gut. "Why not?" I said.

I picked up my rifle from next to the bench and followed Everett to the jeep and got in on the passenger's side. He drove past the guard shack. A Military Police guard stood in the doorway staring at us.

"It's not far from here. Just down town."

Everett pulled the jeep into a lighted alley entrance

next to a large gray stucco building.

"Let's go."

"I'll wait here for you, Everett."

"The hell you will! Get in there, soldier," he ordered cheerfully.

"I'm not going inside."

Everett argued awhile, but he finally realized I wasn't going. "Have it your own way, but you don't know what you're missing." He went inside.

After sitting in the jeep awhile, I carried my weapon and staggered around in front of the long alley. At the far end of the alley where it was dark, three Vietnamese men suddenly appeared. They slinked straight toward me about thirty feet away.

"Get out of here. Didi mau!" I shouted.

Still the men crept forward, smiling, their motives unclear.

"Didi mau!"

They kept coming until they were about fifteen feet away. I fired my weapon on automatic and pumped more than a dozen holes into the hotel wall well above their heads. They ran back into the alley and disappeared. In a few minutes, the US Military Police pulled up in front of the hotel in several jeeps. They handcuffed me and threw me in the back of one of their jeeps. Two MPs went inside the hotel after Everett. The jeep with me sped away. In the passenger's side in the front seat, a huge second lieutenant turned and punched me in the stomach.

"Who do you think you are, Private?" he shouted.

The jeep pulled in front of the Military Police headquarters and the driver pulled me out. The lieutenant grabbed my throat.

I smiled at my youthful tormentor.

The lieutenant held his grip firmly. Finally he relented.

"Lock him up."

I laughed at the lieutenant. "You ought to do something about those pimples, sir."

The lieutenant began punching me in the stomach until the driver stepped in. "Don't hit his face, sir."

MPs locked me inside a holding room, and I fell asleep on the bare floor. In the morning, a captain who was a legal counsel for the Army sat across from me at a square wooden table. A tape recorder, a legal pad and three yellow pencils lay on the table directly in front of the intelligent looking officer.

"Would you like some coffee, Private?" The officer sipped his coffee and looked at me in amusement. "Sounds like you had a wild night last night."

I didn't answer.

"What happened?"

"I got drunk."

"The MPs found you in the alley and they said you'd shot up the hotel. Why'd you do that?" He folded arms. His soft face had a practiced sincere look about it.

"I never fired my weapon," I claimed, my eyes fixed on the officer.

"Well, the MPs said the clip in your weapon only had three rounds in it. How do you account for that?"

"I only took three rounds with me."

The captain sat back in his chair, his eyes twinkled. He twirled his yellow pencil cheerfully. He enjoyed the answer.

"I see. Then how do you account for all the holes in the wall?"

"Beats the hell out of me. I didn't put them there."

The officer wrote out a statement that I read and signed. Charges were filed against me for being drunk and off-limits. The officer collected the papers and shuffled them on the desktop, drumming them several times on the rough wooden surface.

"Captain Woods, your company commander, will be here shortly to take you to Song Cau. You're free to go outside."

Captain Woods soon arrived and ordered me to get in the back seat of his jeep.

"I need to get my equipment at the water point."

"Of course."

The captain took my rifle and the driver drove to the water point. I entered the shack and found Smith drinking coffee at the table.

"What are they going to do to you?" Smith asked.

"Send me to Song Cau," I replied as I collected my gear. "Then I don't know. Throw the book at me I guess."

"Are you okay?" Smith asked.

"I'm a little shaky. It never ends, does it?"

Smith stared at me.

"I told you not to go drinking."

"Yes you did. I should have listened to you."

I shook hands with Smith and left the shack. Smith followed outside to watch us leave.

The captain handcuffed my wrists behind my back. The jeep sped past the hotel and I gazed at the window from which the sniper had fired. We circled the park and headed south down a narrow paved road leading from the small town toward Song Cau. Vietnamese farmers walking their oxen lined the roadway, while women carried pails of water suspended at both ends of wooden yokes. The grinning women walked quickly and gracefully in formation. Their hips flared from one side to the other. A Vietnamese bus had stopped beside the road and the Vietnamese squatted in groups while a few Vietnamese men pissed in the grass a few feet away.

I tried to move into a less painful position, but each movement hurt. The captain saw my discomfort. "Maybe next time you'll make better choices."

Mud and water filled the road in stretches, and the earth smelled rank. On both sides of the road, healthy broad-leaf plants flourished and trees clustered to hide the sun, except in patches where the sunlight streamed through into my uncovered eyes. My predicament reminded me of when I got drafted. I thought about Christ entering Jerusalem on a colt, and it made me smile, but I was afraid and nauseated.

Soon we arrived at the up-hill entrance leading into Song Cau. We passed a South Vietnamese shack, in front of which two middle-aged Vietnamese women stooped before two large wicker baskets. American fatigues swayed on a clothesline.

The jeep accelerated along the flat dirt road as it curved to the right and ran along the northern border of the base. The road ran parallel approximately one-quarter-of-a-mile north of a huge berm. The berm reached above the jungle's tree line in most places. On the south side of the road, I saw rows of tents. Wooden walkways filed through the canvas ranks as though they were blood vessels leading to human organs. Dispersed among the tents, newly constructed wooden barracks housed American soldiers. Fresh skeletons of starter billets further announced the partial Western transformation in Vietnam.

Several huge vehicles blasted by, rocking the jeep, spewing mud and dirt. The traffic included fuel tankers, tractors hauling empty lowboy trailers, several Caterpillar scrapers and deuce-and-a-halves filled with American troops.

As we drove, the captain removed my handcuffs and handed me my weapon. I rocked in the wind from the pressure of the passing vehicles. I could barely hear the captain's voice. He nodded his head forward solemnly. Then he faced the front, poking his dark rimmed glasses against the bridge of his nose with his forefinger.

The road curved south again, passing huge supply yards which contained piles of lumber, mounds of sheet rock, plywood, windows, telephone poles and endless pallets of equipment. The equipment was stacked on top of more pallets filled with metal parts and unrecognizable material. American soldiers scurried around in the yards. One soldier loaded trucks by forklift, while others tied rope over the loads.

The jeep pulled into Headquarters Company 2nd Engineers.

The captain told me to report inside to First Sergeant Goodman. Before I entered the office, I felt some relief seeing an outdoor basketball court with a bright red rim and basket with a fresh nylon net. Inside the building, the company clerk sat typing at the front desk facing the doorway. He was a large passive man with thinning brown hair and an empty sour face. He typed with delicate bleached hands. First Sergeant Thomas L. Goodman sat at his desk to the left. He smoked a cigar and wrote notes in a logbook while looking down his nose through black half-rimmed reading glasses. Finally, he noticed me and he stood up at his desk. He straightened his short powerful frame and expanded his chest. Top's powerful neck forged into broad sloping shoulders and black rugged arms extended through rolled-up fatigue shirt sleeves.

Fierce intelligent eyes set narrowly apart accentuated his broad flat nose and flared nostrils.

Top swiveled the cigar from one corner of his mouth to the other as he eyed me.

"So you're the little whoremaster," he said in quick loud bursts. "Did you have a nice trip?"

"No, First Sergeant."

The clerk stopped typing. Top's voice grew louder, his words more rapid.

"Look at all this paperwork you caused me. You like that?"

"No, First Sergeant."

"Oh yes you do."

"No that's not so," I replied.

"Don't tell me I don't know what I'm talking about. I've seen a thousand just like you." He sat down and put on his reading glasses. Then he took them off. He barked at the company clerk, "Take wonder boy to his platoon and then take him to Sergeant Tromley. And *you*," he poked his finger menacingly at me, "report here 1830 hours for extra duty."

The clerk led me to the water platoon tent where cots were lined up beside one another in two rows that faced one another. Wall lockers placed between the cots on the dirt floor tilted toward the canvas walls and footlockers were positioned at the foot of the cots. I took an empty cot close to the entrance and put my gear in an empty wall-locker.

We left the tent and passed rows of platoon tents, some of which had large tears in their roofs. We reached the working area where approximately twenty-five men labored. Some of the men were laying trusses along the plate of a new two-story barracks. Hammerheads pelted the wooden frame in all directions. Power saws whined through two-by-fours and ripped into the air at higher pitches, their blade guards clamping shut, metal against metal. Sawdust filtered down from the unfinished roof.

The clerk brought me to Sergeant Tromley and I went to work nailing trusses to the plate and plywood to the trusses. At the peak of the roof where the plywood overlapped, I sawed the sheets as close to one another as possible. There were no valleys to build, just a straight ridge.

After chow, I met with the First Sergeant in front of headquarters for my first night of extra duty.

"Three hours extra duty every night," Top said. "You see these sheets of metal spiked to the ground?" He pointed to the ditch near the road. The ditch was at least an eighth-of-a-mile long and shielded on each bank by a solid metal about three-and-a-half feet tall. "They keep mud out of the ditches. Watch me carefully."

Top paced off approximately fifteen feet from where the last four and a half foot spike had been driven behind the fence for support. He guided a metal rod spike into the ground with a few taps from his sledgehammer. His right hand gripped the sledgehammer at the throat close to the head. Once the spike could stand by itself, slanted at an angle, he began to beat the spike into the ground with short powerful strokes. As the spike met the fence at the base, he closed the angle the spike entered the ground. He grunted as he finished nailing it into a vertical position tight against the fence. He ran wire through perforated holes in the metal fence and around the spike.

"See how it works?"

I grinned at the first sergeant whose back was turned to me.

"I guess so."

Sweat beaded on Top's forehead, dripping down his face.

"What do you mean, you guess so? Either you get it or you don't. What the hell's the matter with you?"

I laughed inside.

Top straightened up facing me, his eyes seemed more narrow than usual and his hands were clenched into black fists. I remained quiet, innocent.

"Now watch me closely. Pace off fifteen feet. See those frigging holes in the metal? You nail the spike up against it like so, because you want to wrap the wire through those holes and around the stake."

He put the spike in place and hammered it home. He repeated the same chore except this time he worked more violently. His fatigue shirt became wet with perspiration around his chest and shoulders.

"You get it?"

"Maybe you could do a couple more, I think I'm getting the hang of it."

The flesh at the corner of the first sergeant's eyes wrinkled and he laughed, but tried to catch himself.

"Make sure you get them tight," he said angrily.

By 2200 hours, I had finished for the evening, and at midnight I slept. During the early morning hours incoming rounds exploded in the motor-pool, and I ran to the nearest bunker.

Inside the bunker, the young soldiers breathed stifling air and watched the only light bulb fade on and off. Mortars pounded the bunker's roof repeatedly. Sand filtered down from the ceiling above the light fixture.

A slender sergeant sat in a folding chair in the middle of the bunker, reading a western novel. He peered at me. Wearing a green t-shirt and white cotton boxer shorts, the sergeant sat cross-legged, flapping one of his blue shower thongs against his heel. He exaggerated a nonchalant attitude, turning the pages while the rounds hit.

"This bunker can take direct hits," he said. There's nothing to worry about. Strips of steel are layered between the sandbags in the roof. Mortars can't get in here." He returned to his book. "However, this will go on and off all night, and you will lose sleep."

The Market

The first morning light of Song Cau appeared like a faint memory inside our platoon tent. Before the stirring of the watermen's will, before the rustling of their feet and the wall locker doors rattling, and before the chatter of voices, the gray morning light filtered through the canvas screened windows. The light brushed the soldiers' still faces as they slept in rectangular bunks like well-read letters stored in old shoe boxes.

Smith leaned forward, his bulky arms resting on his knees, his thin blond hair wet from an early morning shower and his fatigues pressed and clean. Quietly, he watched me lying on my back, still, but awake. Smith had recently transferred to Song Cau.

"What's going on?"

"Oh, nothing much," Smith said, annoyed.

"What is it, damn it?"

Smith burst with excitement. "They took you off extra duty, and we're taking a water truck on maneuvers with the 7th Brigade!"

"Maneuvers?"

"That's what they said."

"Who the hell goes on maneuvers in a war? Who got me off extra duty? Balsam?"

Smith shrugged his shoulders.

I arose and took from my wall locker a pair of black milking boots recently bought from a veteran going home.

"We need to get going right now," Smith insisted.

Wrapping a white towel around my waist, I grasped my shaving kit in one hand and opened the canvas door flap. I turned and looked at Smith's clean fatigues. Tauntingly, I said, "You're going to get filthy-dirty loading that truck."

Smith grinned. "I already did it."

"Busy little beaver."

I stepped outside and walked about two hundred yards through deep mud toward a wooden gazebo structure that housed the showers. The walls were boarded around large screens serving as windows. Water flowed from a huge water tank mounted about fifteen feet above the ground outside. I showered, wrapped the towel around my waist, slipped the rubber boots back on and returned to the tent. My legs were nearly free of splattered mud.

As I dressed, Smith said, "We got to get over to 7th Brigade right now."

"Did you sleep at all last night?"

"Not hardly. Sergeant Balsam told me last night we were moving out this morning."

"Why the hell didn't you tell me?"

"I don't know."

I stopped tying my boots, and stared at Smith. "Maneuvers?"

* * * *

The water-purification truck pitched from side to side as I stretched my body and locked my hands behind my head. The deuce-and-a-half moved along slowly within the long convoy.

"Song Cau is a safe place, but it sure gets on my nerves," I said.

"Wright says they make it hard for us on purpose. They hope we get sick of formations and polishing our boots so we don't mind going out in the field," Smith replied.

"I wonder what the hell we're doing now."

"What do you mean?" Smith asked.

I didn't answer.

"I don't know," he shouted happily, "but at least we're moving."

"It's all the same," I said absently.

"I like the 7th Brigade," Smith said happily. "They have bigger trucks than we do. But I'm sick of setting up water points every night when they don't even use our water. And then we go somewhere else and do it all over again."

"It's been a month."

Diesel smoke belched from the rear of a deuce-and-a-half just ahead of us and the fumes poured into our cab. The stench lingered as the water truck slid momentarily on a mound of smooth wet soil formed in the middle of the road. The front wheels jolted into line as they slid into a rut formed by previous traffic. The vehicle moved forward without hesitation.

Rain started to pour through the open windows into the cab and we rolled the windows shut. Water blasted furiously against the windshield, and low visibility forced Smith to slow the truck to a virtual crawl.

I grinned and pointed my finger. "Oh look another tributary."

"I'm going to get me a soda pop," Smith shouted.

The convoy stopped in a small village near a tributary of the Sung Bic and the ordeal began. The first deuce-and-a-half with a trailer attached pulled into the loading area. Soldiers removed the trailer and pushed the trailer onto a turnstile. The trailer rotated around on the turnstile and the soldiers pushed it manually onto a ferry. Next, they loaded the truck onto the turnstile and then into the boat in front of the trailer. Two more vehicles were squeezed in. The ferry chugged slowly across the river, and when it reached the other side, the same procedures were performed in reverse order. The empty ferry chugged back to the convoy to reload. Several hours later, the entire convoy had been transported.

Once the convoy proceeded again, the rain subsided and the sun barely shone through bits of gray clouds. Eventually, the convoy worked across a broad rural landscape. The buildings in the last village seemed cleaner and more cohesive in design, more symmetrical and nearly Western. The unpaved streets were empty.

Farther down the road, an elderly South Vietnamese farmer stood alone on a dike, which extended perpendicular to the roadway and stretched across the middle of a four or five acre rice field. The farmer required no less scrutiny than a city dweller. He sported a gray Ho Chi Minh goatee with its long thin current flapping in the moist breeze. His narrow eyes scanned the movement of men and machinery. Nothing in him stirred. He smiled in his bright blue poncho spanked clean by the rain.

Nearby, other farmers, dressed in drab ponchos by comparison, walked barefooted, stopping along the roadway, facing the convoy. They stooped and smiled cheerfully.

Seven or eight miles west of the village, the convoy pulled into a small compound built to feudal proportions. It consisted of six well-kept white stucco buildings. The convoy parked along both sides of the farm road, and the soldiers waited for instructions. The hamlet appeared to be abandoned.

A large house with a huge back yard and concrete fence stood about three hundred feet away from a smaller house. The property seemed to belong to a chief landowner. A foreman or another man of service probably occupied the little house. Tool sheds and other small buildings lined the road.

The major in charge of the 7th Brigade ordered two riflemen to inspect the main dwelling. The major approached us.

"Set up right here." He pointed to a swamp-like area filled with small pockets of mud and rancid water.

"Sir, it's too hard to pump water here," I said. "The suction side of the pump will keep losing its prime."

"I want drinking water established here tonight, Private."

As the major turned and walked away, his steps bobbed up oddly as though the only energy involved came from his calves.

"I knew he'd do something like that," I said. "Let's find a place to sleep first."

I looked across the street at a building with concrete stairs spread laterally around its entrance. A handful of American soldiers accompanied by a few South Vietnamese soldiers entered the building. The men trudged forward, carrying their weapons and field gear. One American packed a radio. Yellow light flickered from within the building.

"Let's go in there. We can't do any better than that. It's the infantry," I said.

The building's white masonry blended well with a maroon shingled roof squarely pitched. A second, much smaller tier rose in the middle of the roof. Two small narrow sections with rounded roofs and arched eaves joined each side of the second rise.

Inside there was one large room. Several smaller rooms with closed doors lined both walls. The large room joined a sunken den occupied by about fifteen infantrymen. Some of the men talked loudly to one another. Others stood, wrapped in Army towels, hair wet, showered, nerves unwinding. They all spoke easily amongst themselves.

A platoon sergeant talked on the radio, giving directions to another soldier in the field. The static and squawk from the radio echoed inside the room. The field voice crackled over the air, discussing logistics incomprehensible to us. The static finally stopped completely. The tall, thin middle-aged platoon sergeant looked at us inquisitively.

"What's going on, fellows?"

He put a cigarette in his mouth, striking a match, cupping his hands. The sulfur erupted completely and burned itself out before he could draw smoke. Nonchalantly, he succeeded on the second try.

I moved more closely to the sergeant. "Sarge, we're attached to the 7th Brigade. We're watermen. They want us to set up tonight and supply water for tomorrow. Can we sleep here tonight?"

"You bet. Follow me."

He led us to a small room occupied by a German Shepherd guard dog.

"You can sleep here. The dog won't bother you."

The sergeant hesitated in the doorway.

"Do you guys know what this place is?"

"No."

"It's a Buddhist temple."

"Where'd all the monks go?" Smith asked.

"Now you're getting the picture." The sergeant smiled and then added almost delightedly, "This place is crawling. Sleep tight, troops."

"Thanks a lot," I answered.

The sergeant left the room chuckling.

We went outside and unloaded the hard rubber hoses from the truck, connecting the male to female couplings, and we plumbed the water unit. Smith removed the metal meshed stairway and hooked it up in the doorway next to the luxurious shower head. I set up the distribution pump. Smith started the generator and began filling the erdulator cone inside the water purification truck with water. The suction side of the source pump filled with mud, and after several primes, we took turns constantly moving the suction hose to deeper puddles.

After finding a deep pocket of water, I worked inside and assembled chemical slurries. I pinched the plastic feeder lines with metal clamps to calibrate the flow of chemicals.

When the rig was fully operating, Smith pumped processed water from a containment tank into a metal filter that contained diatomaceous rods. As the water pressure dropped, he backwashed, eliminating the dirty water, then he pumped the clean water into a rubber tank outside. The water wasn't perfect but it would have taken much longer to get it exact.

At about 0300 hours we had enough water for the day, so we went to our room and inflated our air mattresses. When we had entered the room, the dog's ears stood up momentarily but his eyes remained sad and disinterested.

"I bet he got drafted too," I said.

Smith didn't reply. He turned his back to the dog and me and fell asleep quickly.

Around 0400 hours a single mortar landed in the yard near the temple. Three American flares lit up the camp. I awoke and gathered my weapon and ammo belt and watched from the open window. Smith remained sleeping. Nothing stirred for several minutes. Then I heard Americans talking in low tones. More flares lit the sky. No other rounds landed in the compound, and I stayed awake until daylight then fell asleep. Around 0700, I awoke and found myself alone in the room.

Smith scurried into the room, loud and jovial. "The major said to take down the water point and get ready to move out."

"It's too much to do."

"That's what I'm trying to tell you." Smith said. "I think the major is evil."

"When did you first realize that?"

"This morning. I don't like him."

We gathered our gear and left the room. Outside, as we began tearing down the equipment, a master sergeant appeared. Dark eyebrows furrowed together on his massive forehead. His square body seemed to intrude into airspace like a blunt object, a useful tool in a fight, a stout weapon.

"The major wants you guys on line in fifteen minutes," he said.

"Well, he better get somebody to help us if that's what he wants," I said angrily.

"I know what you mean. I'll get some guys."

Eventually we disassembled the equipment and loaded the truck. The convoy had already formed and we joined the rear. Nearby an Army Chinook, a large cargo helicopter, strained to lift itself into the air. Airborne, the craft lumbered high across the sky.

The crack of a single enemy Ak-47 that was fired from a strip of jungle close to us ripped into the helicopter's rotary assembly. Black smoke poured from the helicopter and it descended about a mile from the convoy.

The men in the rear of the convoy moved about twenty feet to higher ground to see the chopper blades auto rotate and the craft land near a river in the open valley.

The stout sergeant who had talked to us earlier, said, "We need to get those men out of there, Major. We can do it."

The major fidgeted.

"That's not my responsibility, Sergeant. There's infantry out there, and they will recover those men."

"The infantry came in last night. There's nobody out there," the sergeant snarled.

"Don't differ with me, Sergeant. Order the convoy to move out immediately."

The sergeant stared at the officer.

"What are you waiting for, Sergeant? You have your orders."

The sergeant spit on the ground.

The major bristled but he didn't confront him, instead he shouted at us. "What are you two morons looking at? Get into your truck!"

We waited in our truck while the major barked at other soldiers. I felt nausea build inside my stomach as the convoy pulled out. I felt relieved for not having to go into the valley to fight, but I knew the men in the Chinook would die or be taken prisoner. I felt safe and cowardly.

* * * *

By mid-afternoon the gray light fused into a thicker dreary gray as the convoy entered a fairly large town. The town sprawling, ever breeding, its wrangling Vietnamese culture poured into the streets. People gawking and yakking.

Somewhere in the middle of the town, the convoy jammed into a bottleneck along a muddy road next to a river. One truck and trailer could not maneuver through a concrete arched gateway. In the deep mud, dry ruts had formed earlier in the year and each time the truck driver tried to swing his truck and trailer beyond the gateway, the trailer slid along the greased ruts and slammed into the sturdy columns.

The major stood with his hands on his hips, his impatience mounting.

"What the hell is wrong with your driver, Sergeant? My God, can't your men do anything right?"

"Apparently not, sir," the stout sergeant said with contempt.

The major's legs gave way for an instant like a man on ice. He did a semi-split along two muddied ruts. He regained his balance instantly but the brief loss of control irked him.

"Get someone in that truck who can drive, you idiot!"

Somehow Smith appeared eating peaches from a can and stood between the adversaries.

"Sarge, unhook the trailer. Drive the truck through.

Then push the trailer through."

"Fuck," the sergeant said.

Immediately, one soldier shook the trailer tongue and Smith removed the thick pin. As the men began to straighten the trailer in the road, school let out.

Lines of cute, snobbish Vietnamese schoolgirls strolled by. Their shining black hair resting on large white collars were attached to long white dresses. Their sober small bodies moved along neatly with purpose. Listlessly, the Americans stood in the constant drizzle, wet and curiously mellow, pausing to rest and observe.

Avoiding eye contact, the tiny Vietnamese faces strained, their noses turned upward, little feet walking somehow free from the universe of mud. Quietly, they moved past the groups of soldiers. Then two dreamers straggled into the roadway near the archway; one an awkward skinny girl of about ten years, and the other girl, a plump, slow of pace, older child.

An American from the 7th Brigade, a short stocky young man with red hair and freckles, took the menacing stance of a Western monster. His arms outstretched, hands held above his head with fingers spread and curled, he growled and staggered toward the girls. Frankenstein.

Panic stricken the girls squealed and ran in different directions. The soldier chased the skinny one. Her shrill voice of horror reached an abrupt crescendo and then registered ugly disgust after she had fallen headfirst into a fresh pool of mud.

"Kellum coom cock bick... you," she spit, rising in her soiled white dress, fists clenched, eyes bulging, soldiers laughing. She chased the red headed soldier in circles around a tree and shrub. From her steaming mouth more currents of scathing Vietnamese flowed. All the hair on the left side of her head had matted together into one disturbing clump. Her plump friend pulled her away from the laughter. Stinging anguish pursued them and the fallen one would not be consoled.

Yankee doodle Yankee swine.

Even the major laughed spontaneously and when the laughter had trickled into submission, he entered the conscious flow of events as though he had orchestrated it.

"All right men, let's get on with it. When we get out of here tonight, we'll sleep in dry bunks."

Staring at Smith and me, he ordered us to follow his jeep. It took us nearly forty minutes of maneuvering the water truck and trailer into position before the two vehicles sped along the river road. Eventually we crossed a narrow concrete bridge that arched compactly over the river. We passed several wooden huts bordering an empty area that stretched below the bridge for about one-half an acre. Thick poles held a flat bamboo mat roof pitched above a large portion of the area near an abandoned shack about ten feet from the river.

I didn't understand the layout. Scattered small huts, two to three hundred feet away from the river, converged into the city.

The major stood next to the river. "This yard is sufficient to allow my vehicles ample turn-around space. Position your equipment next to the river, there." He pointed while he talked. Then he put his hands behind his back, interlaced his fingers and stood posing in the light rain.

"We need an infantry point here with us tonight," I

said.

"This is a safe place, Private; this city is on our side. Besides, we're only up the road two miles. My sergeant will be down here this evening to see how you are progressing. You will establish this water point tonight and you will provide plenty of water first thing in the morning." Emphasizing his words with his forefinger shaking in my face, he threatened, "If you fail to provide this support, I will send a report to your Battalion Headquarters."

"We've always supplied the water, sir," I said softly.

Pleased with my tone of voice, the major took his time studying my face.

"Do you know what a levy is?"

I didn't reply.

"I didn't think so," he continued. "A levy is a written tool to induct men into further service, if you will, in perhaps a more active combat role. The infantry often needs men immediately. Men like you get on those lists."

I blinked and looked away from the officer.

"I perceive you actually possess some degree of intelligence, but you need encouragement in directing it respectfully. Perhaps the evenings here will help you reflect on your indolence."

The driver and the major drove away in their jeep.

"What was that all about?" Smith asked uneasily.

"Just what he said."

"You shouldn't of got him started way back there. He's never going to quit bothering us."

"If he's got a problem, it's not with you, Smith."

"You should just leave him alone."

"You're beginning to sound like my mother."

"Well you shouldn't be talking back to him so much."

"I didn't say anything. He left us here because we saw him abandon the men in the Chinook. There's nothing we can do about it now, so let's get the water going and quit crying about it."

Smith sulked.

"I ain't crying about it."

"Okay. Okay. Let's just drop it."

We stood looking at one another briefly until I heard the city squawking again, the Vietnamese voices jabbering, kids and old men shuffling around on the bridge, staring. I put my arm around Smith's shoulder and he looked away immediately.

"We're just overtired, that's all. I'll be more careful. You all right?"

"I'm okay. I'm sorry if I said something..."

"Never mind. Let's just forget it and go to work."

By early evening we had set up the equipment. We had shut down the water point and were both standing near the distribution pump when voices echoed off the water and gunshots suddenly erupted across the river on the other side of the bridge. We ran for cover behind the truck. The gunfire ceased and the voices quieted.

"Let's get out of here," Smith said.

We grabbed our gear and ran upstream to the far end of the open space, where we set up behind the shack next to the riverbank.

The door of the shack had been ripped off its hinges. Piles of waterlogged clothing, broken brown bottles made of thick and imperfectly formed glass, and newspapers were strewn inside the shack on the dirt floor. Vietnam squalor inside Vietnam squalor.

About an hour passed without further gunfire and I told Smith to get some sleep while I watched. Smith curled up in the fetal position and wrapped himself in his poncho liner, his weapon tucked closely beside him. Soon he fell asleep next to the river.

I felt guilty about drawing Smith into this situation. Then I ignored my thoughts and watched bits and chunks of wood float by, drifting toward the bridge. The river smelled rank like dead fish. I stretched my legs and back and then smelled the mud-caked compacted soil and the stench of the river more deeply. Complete darkness began to sift me into deeper feelings of dread.

Occasionally, bursts of gunfire popped from across the bridge. Nausea and adrenalin turned to liquid inside me, like the river lapping against the bank in gentle waves. Slurping sounds, almost peaceful, gentle, mixing inside me, surging into fear.

I strained to see enemy movements everywhere, to feel beyond my senses, to know without reason, to hear without hearing, to become united with the stench and to endure.

Just before daylight, Smith awoke.

"You should have got me up before this."

"I was too wired to sleep, so I let you."

"Did they shoot anymore?"

"Yeah, they sure did. You were out of it."

"Damn, I didn't hear anything," Smith said yawning.

We decided to take turns working the water while one of us guarded. After several hours the yard filled with US Army vehicles pulling water trailers. American voices yelled playfully.

By late afternoon the traffic for the water had died down and Smith sat behind the shack cleaning his weapon. He gave me his M-16 and took mine to clean.

"It's the least I can do since you pulled guard all night."

While he cleaned my clips and rounds, a three-quarter pulled into the yard. Sergeant Balsam got out of the truck after saying something to his driver.

"What are you doing here, Sergeant?" Smith asked happily.

"Come to get you. They want you back in Song Cau. You fucked up."

"What do you mean? I've been here all the time."

"Finance wants your ass up there. Your paperwork all screwed up."

Sergeant Balsam smiled at me. "You look like you enjoying yourself, Garrett."

"Is that what it is?" I replied, feeling the stiffness in my face when I talked.

Balsam laughed from his belly without effort.

"Yeah, you look like you in a movie or something."

"There's been shooting across the river last night and early this morning. Nothing has come our way, but we don't know what's going on," I said.

"Hurry up and get your stuff, Smith, we moving out

right now." Turning to me he added, "7th Brigade be moving out pretty soon too. A day at the most."

"Is the driver staying here with me?"

"No, no. You be here by yourself for the time being."

"Damn it, Sarge, this place is full of gooks."

"They ain't nothing to worry about here. These gooks are friendly."

"They've been shooting here, I told you."

"You'll be okay. I wouldn't ask you to do something I wouldn't do myself. Don't get yourself all worked up over nothing. These people on our side."

He turned away from me and shouted, "Hurry up, Smith, we got to get out of here."

"What's your big hurry," I asked.

"In a minute, Sarge," Smith called back.

"What you doing over there, fool?"

"Getting Garrett's stuff."

Turning to me, Balsam said, "I see you got yourself a servant these days."

"It's not like that."

"Don't lie to me, Garrett. You got that hillbilly doing everything for you."

"No way."

"What you call it then?"

"If it were up to him he wouldn't leave me here alone."

"There you go again. Hurry up, Smith, let Garrett pick up his own shit."

Smith tossed the clips to the ground where he had spread out an old towel. Nervously, he gathered the clips and loose ammo and put them inside my ammo box. Locking a clip inside my M-16, he hurried toward the sergeant.

"I'm ready to go, Sarge. Here's your gun, Garrett."

"Man," Balsam said in exasperation, "didn't they teach you nothing? It ain't his gun; it's his weapon. You hopeless."

Balsam stood there with his arms folded in front of him. He stared at me briefly. "Just do your job and keep your eyes open. It just be another day."

"I haven't slept for days, and this place is crawling," I replied, my voice trailing off.

"Let's go, Smith!" Balsam started to walk away.

"Would you ask the major to send a couple infantrymen down here tonight? But don't tell him I asked you," I said.

He stopped and scowled. "I'll do what I can." He seemed to be mulling things over in his large head. "You not getting along with the major? That it?"

"No, it's not that. It's just that he'd listen to you because you're a sergeant and you have more experience than I do. That's all."

Balsam liked that.

"Like I said, I'll see what I can do."

I looked at Smith and a twinge of guilt registered in his face. He lowered his eyes for a second and began to speak, but I stopped him.

"Don't worry about it. I'll see you in Song Cau."

"I don't want to go back to Song Cau in the middle of the night," Balsam shouted impatiently, "Get your ass a move on, Smith."

"I'll talk to the major for you," Balsam shouted from the truck as it pulled out of the yard.

Smith waved good-bye from the back of the truck as a large crowd of Vietnamese, mostly kids, scattered from the truck's path. His blond head disappeared from my sight and I thought it seemed as though he was never there. The engine whined and the truck accelerated along the narrow passage past the crest of the small bridge.

I slung my weapon over my shoulder, picked up my bandolier, ammo and ammo box and carried them to the water truck. I draped the bandolier over the fuse box inside the erdulator van and I set the ammo box down on the floor drain.

Moments later a US Army truck hauling a water trailer pulled into the yard. I left the erdulator, started the distribution pump and talked to the driver. As soon as the driver left, I shut the pump off and returned to the erdulator. Vietnamese had ransacked my belongings and had taken my ammo, clips and C-rations.

I raged briefly, but stopped abruptly and acted calmly. Glancing in the direction of the bridge, then along the river and near the shack, I checked to see if anyone had been watching me. Vietnamese milled around the bridge, but they did not look in my direction nor seem to be interested in me. I continued to force myself to act calmly while I scanned the erdulator looking for ammo. Then I realized the only ammo I had was in my weapon, so I released the clip. Two rounds. Smith hadn't filled the clip.

I picked up my gear and walked next to the river, sat down and waited. No other Americans came. It grew dark. I tried to think pleasant thoughts, to reminisce, but the images in my head would disappear as soon as they formed and nausea flooded me. I told myself that I was really in a safe place no matter what I felt. I told myself that I was being too dramatic and that I'd be okay. Then I'd remember I only had two rounds and then I'd stay with that for a while. I studied the shifting night movements, the shadows and I listened for sounds. The silence created its own sound. A humming sound. It seemed better to dwell with the fear in the present although part of me knew there was nothing I could do about anything. I thought about the gooks sneaking up on me if I fell asleep and how they would slit my throat or shoot me. Stay awake. One round for them. One for me.

It went on like that until about two hours before daylight and then I held my weapon in my right hand and I lay on my back beneath the bamboo roof. I closed my eyes and told myself: "Take the safety off. Leave it on. If they shoot me or stab me I can't do anything about it any way. Put the safety on. I might shoot myself in my sleep."

* * * *

I knew they were there. It was too quiet. I could feel their eyes staring at me. I could hear their boats rocking in the water, the water lapping against the riverbank. I opened my eyes and saw men, women and children waiting silently. Their boats were filled with produce. They didn't disturb me because I had fallen asleep with my finger wrapped around the trigger of my M-16.

I got up feeling the familiar stiffness in my body and the soreness in my eyes. I felt the safety and it was on.

I laughed. I was still alive.

The Vietnamese did not move in their boats. They watched me get up and walk beside the river and lean down to splash water into my face. Finally, a tall girl about eleven years old got out of a boat and walked close to me, about ten feet away. She carried a pot and she dipped it into the river, never once taking her eyes off me.

While I splashed water into my face, sensing the people being quiet in their funny boats and the little girl being brave, I suddenly turned my face toward her and made three short loud snorts like a hog. She jumped straight into the air. She screamed. The people in the boats laughed. She waved her arms. Angry and embarrassed, her face twisted into odd expressions as she jabbered in short steady bursts. Her people continued to laugh and then they began unloading their produce and fish to sell what then became obviously a market under a bamboo roof. It grew quiet again except for the sound of feet in the water. Every now and then they'd look over at me and they'd smile.

And I smiled back.

Splendid Little Cakes

A month after I had returned from the river
and maneuvers, the 2nd Engineer Battalion
was housed in wooden barracks. Four wooden
walls and the Army's regimental scheme of things:
the formations, inspections, military "courtesies,"
the little tasks and forced behavior all cried out to
establish order in the day-time universe. But the night
belonged to the Viet Cong.

The mortars flew often, as many as three different
times a night, and stopped unpredictably for days
and even weeks. The explosions had sifted into
the soldiers' unconscious minds and lay dormant,
unseemly wounds. The anticipation of attack became
another form of attack, and night became the enemy.
Every now and then a mortar or a rocket actually
killed a man.

And so it was around 0200 hours when I awoke to
a rocket ripping into the mess hall about twenty-
five feet from my barracks and bunk. I heard the
lively footsteps pounding upon the second floor and
trampling down the wooden stairways constructed
outside the walls of the barracks. And as I hit the
rough concrete floor running, between the steel beams
staggered in the aisle, I heard a new guy running

headlong into one of the steel beams behind me. The familiar steel twang echoed just before the recruit's familiar agonizing moans.

Quickly outside, I crossed the sandy space to come to rest within a huge well-lit musty bunker. Sergeant Balsam sat inside on a wooden bench, waiting. He appeared cavalier about having reached safety first, as though he considered himself to be an exceptionally wise and alert warrior.

He leaned forward, his legs crossed.

"What took you so long, Garrett?"

"You must be sleeping in here," I replied.

"It just seem that way to you. Confidentially, I knew this one coming before it go in the tube. No thud or nothing. I just come in here. I could feel it."

The sergeant chuckled and tilted his face into the light.

"You must be psychic," Wright said as he sat down too close to Balsam on purpose.

Balsam glared at Wright and edged his butt along the wooden bench, his body swaying and moving only a few inches away.

"I know I be getting psychic," Balsam continued.

"I still don't know how you got in here so fast. It was a rocket," I said.

"Sarge got a new haircut. It looks like they put a rice bowl on his head," Smith said in a loud voice.

"Gooks don't have rice bowls big enough to fit his head," Wright shouted.

"Keep talking Wright and you find your ass in a world of hurt. You be in a firebase you never come back."

The light bulbs flickered inside the bunker. A mortar had hit the roof. A few minutes passed and then we heard heavy footsteps just outside the nearest bunker entrance. A stout sergeant swaggered in, a big strapping Mexican who ran the security platoon. His day job kept him on the roads some of the time providing fire power for convoys. But mostly, he led the Flame Platoon into direct combat almost daily and he had more combat experience than anyone in the bunker. He let everyone know it too. Apparently, he had been standing outside all the time during the rocket and mortar attack.

"They killed Swenson," he said with humor in his voice.

"Who?" Balsam asked.

"The fucking cook," he said. "You know the one everybody hates. He died cooking bread, man." Pausing briefly, he sneered at Balsam.

"What you doing in here, guy?" he said, and then expanded his chest the way a woman would if she had big breasts and wanted to show them off. Then he posed in the bunker holding his arms and fists a certain way that made him look like a boxer. He sneered and left without waiting for Balsam to answer.

We looked at Sergeant Balsam who began to fidget with his white towel. He sponge dried his face repeatedly.

"You know the cook he's talking about?" I asked Wright.

"Yea, that hostile jerk," he said happily.

"Everybody hate that honky," Balsam added.

"Maybe that killed him," I said.

Soon the news spread in the bunker about the dead

cook and a trickle of laughter erupted. The men had resented seeing so much of the surly cook dispensing food when he was alive. His ugly mood and self-contempt had gone before him like a cloud. All the other cooks hated him too, and because of that, a solution arose the same way a missile flies across the dark sky.

Put him on night duty and make him the baker of little cakes, I imagined the First Sergeant thinking. It would resolve the personality conflicts. Isolate the bastard. Cook at night and sleep him during the day. He certainly made splendid little cakes.

I remembered last seeing the cook alive while he was having a fit one late morning while soldiers were hammering nails into the eves above his domicile. The cook stood outside his space in his green boxer shorts with earplugs inserted into small ears and some kind of eye mask propped up on his forehead. He appeared faint, drawn up, ghost like and he was shouting. There was something pathetic about him, a desperation that weakened his delivery. The soldiers sensed it too, and they laughed at him and they hammered more fiercely.

"What a stupid way to die," Wright said.

"Any way you die is stupid," Smith said.

"What do you know about it?" Wright answered sharply.

"What's there to know? Today you're alive, and tomorrow you're dead," Smith replied happily.

"That's what I mean about you," Wright said in exasperation. "Just say anything and make sure you don't think about it first. It's always how much air do we have in the truck tires, or how many more gallons of water do we have to purify before we can go home. Shit like that all the time. Don't you ever think about anything like everybody else?"

Balsam giggled.

"Smith just a country boy, Jeffrey Wright. It ain't his fault he never grow up in San Francisco."

"Why are you mad at me?" Smith asked. "I never did anything to you. If you don't like what I say then don't listen to me."

"Like I had any choice."

"What is bugging you, Wright?" I asked.

"What do you think? Doesn't he ever get on your

nerves?"

"No."

"Why do you let him hang around you all the time?"

"You got it all wrong, Wright, I'm hanging around him."

"You're as screwed up as he is."

"Oh, please like me."

"What do you mean you never did nothing to me?" Wright asked Smith. "What about the time when you yanked my blanket off me and made me think the colonel was still there?"

A sinister smile crossed Smith's face. "You can dish it out, but you can't take it."

"You sound like a little kid."

"You're not all there, if you ask me," Smith said. "If you were all there, you still wouldn't be all there."

Wright looked bewildered. He lit a cigarette. "What the hell's that supposed to mean?"

"He means, if you were all you could be, it wouldn't be enough," I answered, and I laughed.

Wright grinned. "That wouldn't be too good would it?"

"I wouldn't think so."

Eventually the mortars stopped and we headed back to the barracks to sleep. We passed the "heads," five men in a row, passed out in their bunks, likely drugged from any assortment of grass, heroin, alcohol and barbiturates. They had never left the barracks during the mortar attacks.

About half-an-hour later, the mortars started up again and we ran the same drill, except this time the new guy avoided all the steel posts.

Eleven Bravo Invocation

Eleven Bravo Invocation

Please save us from mayhem

And escort us still living

Through harsh green thickets

Of sprawling lime jungles

Where life walks on brave legs

Oh please none be mangled

Be lost or be torn

Where faces fly by us

In the nights of our thinking

As we sleep under stars

Mosquitoes to share

And then there's the whisper

We hear it like humming

But the others find rest

Within four wooden walls

Let us wade through this time

With only brief sorrow

May our minds remain strong

And think nothing of sinking

So low in the distance

So low as our graves.

* * * *

For two weeks, Brooks, a skinny seventeen-year-old, and I worked a water point near the rear of a small, muddy firebase. Behind us, the first of several, long, narrow bunkers stretched straight across the base. Coils of concertina wire separated the base from a village, surrounding us like a horseshoe. Several American tanks faced the open space—a field gently sloping downward for about two hundred yards, merging into solid jungle.

"I'm going into town," Brooks said.

He didn't know the war intruded into the everyday and that there was no every day. We were always attached to other units, attached to strangers.

"Take somebody with you."

"I don't know anybody."

"Then stay put."

"Then I'll make friends with somebody."

He had the look of a bored "killer." Concussion grenades were tied to his ammo belt. His helmet was cocked back on his head, a .45 caliber pistol slung from his hip, a cigarette dangled from his mouth and he carried his M-16 with an aloof menace.

"Why don't you do that? Go make friends with somebody and then bring them back here. This I got to see."

He looked puzzled and walked off.

About an hour later, on my way to chow, I saw a sergeant muckled on to the neck of a squirming Vietnamese. The sergeant shouted questions in Vietnamese. The Vietnamese pleaded. The sergeant shoved a .38 revolver into the man's mouth, pulled back the hammer and asked the same questions again. When he yanked the revolver out, the Vietnamese must have told him what he wanted to know. The words poured out with teeth and blood. I walked past the scene wishing I hadn't seen it.

When I returned to the water point, Brooks hadn't found a friend, but it didn't matter. Another sergeant approached me.

"We're going to get attacked," he said.

"When?"

He laughed. "If we knew that it wouldn't be much of an attack, now would it? I'm telling you so you'll be ready."

"Do you know how many?"

"No. We just know they're coming."

With that he left and nausea stayed. Nausea and dread stayed awake in me for days, until into the mid-afternoon of the fifth day, when a three-quarter pulled into the yard with men from my platoon. Smith and Wright jumped down from the bed and Bates got out from the driver's side. Smith was punching my shoulder when I recognized John Everett approaching me from the passenger's side. Corporal Everett now.

"Looky who's here," Everett said. "Damned if it ain't Garrett."

"Everett."

I started to tell them I was glad to see them and that we were expecting to get hit, when mortars began pounding the firebase. We ran to the nearest bunker where I put on my helmet and flak vest and gathered my weapon and ammo. I noticed Smith had taped some of his magazines together by threes. Two up and one down.

Brooks began to shake and twitch. His young eyes open to panic and closed to everything else. Everett slapped him twice, yelling at him and shaking him. Bates removed Brooks' grenades and took his weapons. Mortars kept hitting the base. American M-79s popped and automatic weapons cracked from different directions, in unison and in consecutive volleys.

"If they get in, they'll throw grenades inside the bunkers," I told Smith. "We need to get on top. Untape your clips."

"Why?"

"Rounds will jam. Clips are too heavy."

I felt the fear of knowing we'd be open to mortars and could get overrun. This could be it. Bates was calming Brooks and Wright while Everett acted tough but stayed inside. They ignored us or pretended to ignore us. It didn't matter. Smith and I went outside, climbed to the top of the bunker, pulled sand bags together around us for cover and waited. The sense of fear submerged into nonbeing, coated over with a quiet, clear awareness. Heavy gunfire in the front of the base sent clouds smelling of sulfur and fog past our point. A slight drizzle continued. We heard a few voices shouting, but mainly automatic weapons and sporadic incoming mortars. Nothing from the tanks. We scanned the areas of the village around us and closely watched the front. Ten maybe fifteen minutes passed and then there was silence, accentuated by fog and the last drifting smell of sulfur. We stood up and looked down the line of bunkers and saw officers slowly emerging. Their heads bowed in shame, seeing us standing top side, two privates having met what they did not. I felt pride spiral up within me, and soon mixed with noticeable contempt. The men from our platoon appeared, led by Everett. He stared at me momentarily and then turned his back on me.

American infantrymen appeared everywhere. And we heard from one, who had been at the front, that a sizable bulk of the enemy attacked straight up the open field, straight into American gunfire; that Charlie must have been high on weed and stupid in the afternoon daylight.

After things settled down, Everett and I stood together.

"I heard you'd be here maybe another month," he said.

"Are you in the water platoon now?" I asked.

He didn't answer.

"I'm sorry they demoted you because of Chung Quyen, but… I don't know if you ever heard what happened?"

"It wasn't your fault. Is that it?" he replied.

"In some ways of course it was. But looking at it another way, I told you I was seeing double."

"Hmm."

"There were gooks in the alley. I had to shoot."

"That's the way it goes."

"Why did you guys come here?" I asked.

"We're checking all the water points."

"Guess you weren't expecting all this."

"I seen worse."

I smiled to myself, thinking he had stayed inside the bunker.

"We're supposed to bring Brooks back with us. This is a secure firebase so you'll go it alone for a while," Everett said absently.

"Fine."

The watermen left.

Smith waved from the back of the truck.

A few days later, the water source dried up. I moved the truck out into the open space where we had been attacked. I had the rig running smoothly in a few days, filling the 3000 gallon clean water storage tank. One afternoon, infantrymen, loaded down with weapons and light gear, began to board choppers, landing a couple hundred feet from my point. Chopper after chopper landed to retrieve and deliver the soldiers into as many LZs it would take until the enemy "*engaged*" them. They moved in a strange deliberateness, a distorted resignation—their thoughts incalculable. I watched about forty men pass before me like workers plodding off toward factories. Several days later about thirty returned. They were indescribably exhausted—figures melted into mud-caked fatigues. Slowly, as they approached me, one asked to be hosed with water from my supply. One after another, I hosed each down with purified water and to a man they thanked me.

That night I removed my boots, washed my feet and fell asleep inside the erdulator van next to the metal cone. Mortars landed, and I ran bootless toward a newly built bunker. My left bare foot stepped on concertina wire. Four prongs stabbed in, four prongs popped out in a ripple. Two days later my foot was so swollen and infected that I couldn't put on my boot, so they sent Wright to replace me and told Smith to drive me back to Song Cau.

"How come you had your boots off?" Smith asked.

"I'm exhausted. I should have stayed inside the erdulator because a mortar probably couldn't penetrate the walls anyway. I don't know what the fuck I'm doing anymore."

"Think you'll get a purple heart?"

"Got a purple foot. I need a vacation."

"Let's go to Vung Tau on In-Country R&R!" he shouted.

"Okay, as soon as I heal."

What Orders?

Top approved our three day In-Country R&R request—Rest and Relaxation. Smith and I decided to leave one day earlier so we could gain an extra day. We carried no weapons. In the morning, the Navy loaded ten of us vacationers onto one of their troop carriers. Sailors inspected our boots and fatigues for mud because they had scrubbed the boat immaculately. The hollowed out lower deck seated the passengers and the upper deck manned a .50 caliber machine gun.

The boat departed on the Song Bic, and long before it journeyed into the South China Sea, I was asleep on my back on the upper concrete deck. Several hours passed and I stayed asleep.

Just before we reached Vung Tau in the late afternoon, the sailors amused themselves by waking us up and making us put on life preservers. They said there was a tidal wave coming. Exhausted, we obeyed before we realized they were screwing with our heads.

On land, carrying our light baggage, Smith and I headed for the gate. An elderly Vietnamese woman and a woman who was probably her daughter saw us passing before them. The old woman cupped her mouth, her body trembled and her eyes looked terrified. The younger woman supported her from collapsing, both arms holding her; the old woman's knees buckling. Smith didn't see it, but I realized the old lady recognized the 2nd Infantry Division patch on our shoulders and it must have triggered a brutal memory. Perhaps a 2nd Division encounter, meant to capture the hearts and minds of the South Vietnamese, somehow turned into the slaughter of the innocents. It only takes one psychopath or two per platoon, and they existed.

At the gate, a young MP ordered the absurd.

"Let me see your orders."

"What orders?" I asked.

"You have to have orders otherwise I can't let you in."

"Let us in?"

"R&R orders!"

"We don't have any."

"I can't let you go into town without orders."

"What are we supposed to do, sleep here on the

ground? How are we supposed to get back?"

"Where you from?"

"2nd Infantry Division."

The MP sighed.

"Just let us go. What the hell difference does it make?"

The MP gave us directions to the transit barracks.

"Go ahead, you stupid fuckers."

We reached the barracks, put our bags in wall lockers and were met by friendly total noncombatants; men assigned tours in the resort town. They asked us questions we didn't answer.

"Where's the mess hall? And where can we get a drink," I asked.

We ate, and soon it became night.

Smith and I walked to an empty bar and drank beer for about two hours and later we went to a different bar with the latest in entertainment: three scrawny worn out Vietnamese women soliciting like-minded Vietnamese men. No American soldiers were present. The women wore only black panties and brightly colored tank tops cut just below their breasts. Thin legs poked out of panties covering flat surfaces where rear ends used to be. There was no music and the women kept walking around several men sitting on stools. The women giggled and pinched the men. Sometimes they'd stare at Smith and me, sitting by ourselves at a distant table, drinking, but they knew better than to come near us. The bar smelled of old beer, filth and squalor.

"What are we doing?" I finally asked Smith who seemed to be fascinated.

"What?"

"Let's get the hell out of here and get some sleep."

We stepped outside and were immediately arrested by MPs. Curfew. They hauled us off in jeeps to their central office where they asked us for our orders, wanted to know our names and what unit we came from. I explained that we were with the 2nd and had come without orders even though we were approved for leave. They took us outside and put us in an approximately fifteen-by-fifteen-by-eight foot corrugated metal box used for cargo shipping. It served as a holding tank. Inside the cell a cut out opening existed in a wall near the ceiling, not big enough for a man to crawl through but space enough to provide air.

The first person I saw inside the cell was an American civilian dressed in a crumbled, robin egg blue suit, dirty white shirt and dark blue tie. He looked silly but smiled and then wanted to know what had we done to get there.

"I murdered a civilian," I replied.

He kept chattering away about what he was doing in Vung Tau, something phony about the CIA.

There were three other American soldiers in there as well, and they never said a word. Mid way through the early hours I had to piss, so Smith and two soldiers lifted me up so that I was horizontally aligned to the open space. Of course I withdrew into a social phobic trance and could not go, so they lowered me to the floor. A few minutes later I pleaded, and they repeated the same exercise, military pressing me for what seemed like eons until finally I succeeded.

About 0700 the MPs unlocked and opened the cell door. The day sergeant in charge of the MPs looked at Smith and me in disgust, and said, "Why didn't you tell these guys where you were from?"

"I did. I explained everything."

"Shit!" he said.

He took us inside his office, drew up some paperwork and continued to be honestly upset on our behalf. He kept us there about half-an-hour and then he called our First Sergeant. Top wanted to speak to me.

"You miserable little son-of-a-bitch! What in the fuck is wrong with you, Garrett? We've been through all this shit before. Tell me this isn't happening."

"We shouldn't have gone without our orders, Top. I…"

"Oh, that explains everything. Get your skinny ass back here. I'm warning you. You'll end up in Long Bien Jail this time as sure as I'm a mad black angry mother fucker. Do you hear me, you little bastard?"

He hung up.

"What did he say?"

"He wished us a pleasant trip back."

"That's a relief," Smith replied.

Smith and I went back to the transit barracks, showered, shaved and changed into the only clean fatigues we had. We ate and headed for a bench that faced a helicopter pad where we waited for a ride to Song Cau.

We waited and waited.

One at a time we'd run to get candy, potato chips and soda pop, while the other guarded the possibility of a ride, as if one could hold an aircraft for the other if it ever arrived. Hours passed. What had been two refreshed soldiers now had become two bored young men with greasy film covering stubbly faces. Nothing landed. We headed back to the barracks, ate, slept and started another day.

Helicopters landed but nothing going anywhere near Song Cau. On the third day we went to the dock where the Navy had dropped us off, but they had already left. We returned to the pad and finally—four days later—a helicopter took us to Long Bien. It wasn't Song Cau but at least we were getting closer.

"I got to call Top."

My nausea reached the same level before we had

recently been attacked by the Viet Cong.

"It won't be so bad. You'll see," Smith said.

"So you call him."

"No. He knows you better."

I called.

"Top, let me explain."

"Of course. There must be some explanation for all this. You certainly heard me when we last spoke. Isn't that so, Private Garrett?

"Yes, Top, but…"

"But, but, but… Enjoy yourself. Have a good time and come back soon. I'm looking forward to seeing you."

He hung up.

Later in the afternoon, a chopper dropped us farther away from Song Cau but at a larger base from which we assumed more traffic would flow.

Ten days passed and nothing headed for our base. We stayed in transit billets doing nothing for the Army. No duty of any kind. We drank in the enlisted men's club at night, and I shot baskets during the day. Smith did Smith things, like inspecting insects, or lingering to smell the new canvas platoon tents, or asking why there weren't any dogs or cats in Vietnam.

A C-130 cargo plane loaded us up and flew us to Song Cau one day later. We were strapped in when it made an awful landing. The craft lost lift at least ten feet above the surface of the run way and hit the ground so hard it should have split the plane in half. It bounced and hit the ground again.

We had to walk about two miles to face Top after being AWOL eighteen days. We walked and didn't speak. Smith didn't seem to have any fear. It were as though he lived so in the present moment that the present moment didn't affect him. So it seemed, until we entered Top's office at Headquarters.

Top dropped his pen, removed his reading glasses, stood, put his hands on his hips and said, "Well, well, here they are at last. Our very own. And how should I put this? We're so delighted you've decided to join us."

Smith and I lowered our heads and looked at the floor.

"This is the dumbest stunt you've ever pulled, Garrett. You've got shit for brains. What can you possibly say for yourself?"

A long pause.

"Speak up! I'm dying to hear."

"I just fucked up, Top."

He began to raise his voice to a level I could not imagine possible and spoke words at a speed I had never experienced.

"Time to fuck up again is that it, Private Garrett? Is that all you got? And Smith, you don't even exist. You're just another simpleton, floating along in a universe of shit."

And then his voice, though loud, lost gravity. It didn't belong to him and it didn't belong for us.

"You're on extra duty every day until I leave this miserable hole, and you will carry my bags to the company jeep the day I leave. Now get the hell out of my office and take a shower. You stink."

Smith and I looked at each other in disbelief. No Long Bien Jail. Nothing.

"I said get out of here!"

We showered, ate, shopped at the PX, drank beer at my bunk in the night, told our stories to the others and received a visitor, the company clerk. Top's typist.

He came smiling.

"You should have heard him. All day long he kept saying your name. 'Garrett.' Then he'd laugh and kept laughing. He'd say it over and over again: 'Garrett, that crazy, skinny son-of-a-bitch!' And laugh, he laughed all afternoon."

Trash Run

The next afternoon, Wright and I were assigned trash-run. We loaded up mostly metal parts from the S-4 yard, parts we couldn't identify. Paper, cardboard, plastics, worn canvas covers and old wooden pallets, among other things filled the back of our deuce-and-a-half. Wright drove the truck while I sat in the passenger's seat with my M-16 tucked under my arm.

"You guys were lucky," Wright said. "It's a wonder Top didn't send you to LBJ."

"I know. Don't think I haven't thought about it. He had the right to court martial us."

"He didn't even put you on extra duty?"

"When I first came here, I was on extra duty and Top used to mess with me. He saw it didn't bother me working late. Guys always gave me beer like I was against the man and all that. Top saw me painting the water tank, so he put that goofy kid up there with me."

"What goofy kid?"

"I don't know. That guy who wanted to marry a Vietnamese sandbagger."

"Ohhh! That guy. How did he get in the Army?"

"How'd *you* get in the Army?"

Wright smiled but he was annoyed.

"Well Top put that uncoordinated little bastard up there so I'd be afraid he'd knock me off the frigging tank. That tank is about twenty feet high! I lost my temper and told him get down and hold the ladder. Top walks by and sees the kid holding the ladder, but the only thing is it's nailed to the wooden structure."

Wright's blatting laughter hurt my ears.

"Top walks by smiling, so I said to him, 'You're the bastard who put that moron up here just to piss me off.' He made a face like he's getting a big kick out of everything, but pretending not to hear me swearing at him."

"I'd be afraid of Top."

"You should be. Remember Michaels?"

Wright nodded.

"He pissed Top off, and Top sent him to the Flame Platoon. That's a death sentence." I paused. "Don't think that didn't cross my mind."

We pulled into a flat open field where no person stirred in our forward vision. Paper blew in the air and lay strewn over the area. The terrain sloped downward from our position as we moved slowly straight ahead to the end of the field toward the dump.

"How are we going to unload all this crap?" Wright asked. His voice pitched high and strained.

"We forgot to bring shovels and a push broom," I said absently.

Wright stopped the truck.

I could hear yelling, so I looked back and saw a pack of about forty kids running barefooted toward our truck. Before we could respond, the truck rocked as they climbed all over the bed. I could hear their shrill excited voices. At times angry, arguing over the spoils of war. Wright and I stayed in the truck, resigned thankfully that we didn't have to unload anything. Like swarms of locusts they devoured the entire load, hauling just about everything away within minutes.

They sped away as quickly as they came.

I opened the passenger's door and saw a grenade lying on the running board. I jumped down and grabbed it, pulled back my arm to throw it, the grenade next to my head, when I felt pain like waves of electricity surging throughout my being and hurting; thinking it would explode in my face. I threw it and watched it roll down the sloped field until it stopped. By this time Wright knew what had happened and we both waited for it to explode.

It didn't.

"Want to go look at it?" Wright asked.

"What poke it with a stick? Let's just get the hell out of here."

We drove back to the base and Wright kept taking side glances at me and smiling.

"You should see your face," he said.

"I'm lucky *you* can."

Then I added, "And so are you. If that thing had gone off it would have taken you out too."

"Okay Snow White."

He was right about that. I couldn't feel my face and the rest of me felt numb and dizzy.

We pulled into the motor pool where it bordered the end view of the barracks and approached a straight line of about ten fifty gallon barrels cut in halves. They were placed on the side of the road. The man who cut them with a welding torch worked every day for months burning human waste so he'd never have to leave the base. It was his purpose; his chosen Vietnam occupation. What the hell would he tell his kids? "What did you do in the war, Daddy?"

Survival wouldn't be enough.

The barrel halves fit beneath the toilet holes and when they were filled with waste, he'd open the wooden flaps on the outside, pull the barrel-halves out and burn the waste. He'd pour some gasoline and diesel fuel into the barrels and stoke the flames all day. The smoke would rise up smudging his olive complexion into a dark discernible hue.

Wright, without any forewarning, no expression at all, drove the deuce-and-a-half over most of the barrels; crushing them into useless flattened metal objects.

We both cracked up.

Finally, I told him to park the truck.

"Hurry up!"

When we got out I said, "Michaels—the reason Top put him in the Flame Platoon was when he had shit detail he filled one of the barrels with gasoline and lit it. Flames flew twenty feet into the air and Top saw it. Said he'd fix his ass and he sent him to Flame."

Wright straightened up. He actually expressed momentary concern.

"So, don't tell anyone you did this."

He nodded solemnly.

We killed some time in the barracks and then I went to Headquarters to see what else we were supposed to do. As I entered the side door I saw fecal man standing before Top's desk. The man held his jungle hat in his hands in front of him, standing there timidly. Top, intensely concentrating on his paperwork, didn't immediately notice the man. When he finally looked up, his body recoiled in disgust. The man said someone ran over his barrels and he wanted justice, but Top exploded when he saw the man's soiled complexion. In fierce anger he ordered him to get the hell out of his office. The man left dejectedly and Top sat down, still highly agitated and talking to himself. I left, purposely unnoticed, went back to my barracks and sat between Wright and Everett on Wright's bunk.

I didn't say anything because Everett was there, but I mused over what I had just seen. Private Brooks ambled in front of us. His eyes said everything. They looked at us but didn't focus. He was like a spirit temporarily occupying a body that didn't belong to him and in his right hand he held a .38 revolver.

He pointed the weapon at me and said, "I'm going to kill you. All of you." He repeated it again in a monotone voice.

Wright and Everett looked at me.

I said, "Think about it, Brooks. They'll send you to LBJ, and you're just a little guy. The prisoners will rape you. All of them."

He lowered his eyes momentarily.

"You know the battalion formations we have? After six months in LBJ they'll ship you back here and parade you around the battalion. All the men will know what happened to you."

I looked at him sorrowfully.

"Then they'll make you finish your tour. You'll be back in the same place you're in now. So why don't you just give me the .38 and we'll forget about it."

He slumped forward, blinked slowly and then he handed me the revolver. Everett jumped him, threw him down and started slamming his head against the concrete floor. I pulled Everett off him, shouting, "You'll kill him!"

"Nobody's going to threaten me with a gun. Nobody. I will kill him!"

"Leave him alone. He's not well."

Everett stared at me but recovered himself somewhat. Brooks drifted away, his face bleeding.

"What's wrong with him?" Wright asked.

"Too much stress. It's too much," I replied.

We stayed quiet for some time. Everett calmed down completely.

"Soon we're going to Khong Dan," he said firmly.

"Who's going?" Wright asked.

"You're going first, then Garrett, Bates, Smith and me. Maybe Brooks."

After a while Everett and Wright left.

I stayed on the bunk thinking it didn't matter, just another day to erase from my calendar. My only purpose was to survive, like the guy who had slaved over the barrels that were crushed into worthless metal. His will to meaning briefly disturbed, but he will be all right in the morning. Maybe he will hum a tune or two while he works, reassured that he belongs to a cause greater than himself. There will be something noble about his tour. One day he will look back on the war, because he will survive it, and he will be so proud of himself for having served his country. But he will need to lie about the job he chose for himself. For that no one could blame him. He'll choose a more respectable title, like sanitary inspector under the direct supervision of the Medical Corps. And he will try to cleanse his soiled complexion, but it will stay with him forever.

The incident rotated into routine Song Col. For two weeks we drank beer every night into the early morning hours. Nights became days and mortars kept us awake, as though the Cong knew exactly when we slept.

One morning Bates drove. Everett sat up front. Smith, Brooks and I rode in the back of a three-quarter. We reached Khong Dan late morning to find Wright and two recruits working the water point. Two systems were set up, and the new men needed more instruction. More men were needed to rotate shifts to meet the demand. We settled in for a couple days teaching them.

The last day I went to chow alone and on my way back I saw the watermen standing in the yard. They seemed separated, resigned and they bore a grimness I could see in their stances and energy. I noticed Smith and Wright were not among them.

"Where's Smith?"

"He's inside," Everett said.

"What happened? What's going on?"

Everett spoke with a measure of disdain.

"Wright got himself burned up. A second lieutenant ordered to take a shower. The generator's been running all day." He paused and added, "Wright didn't use the shot glass to prime it. He took a five gallon gasoline can and poured it all over the generator. It exploded. Inflamed is the word for it. They just medevaced him."

"Did it get his eyes?"

"I don't rightly know what it got. Except he was pretty fucked up."

He smirked.

I went inside and sat beside Smith on his bunk. He had been crying.

"What Wright ever do to deserve that?" he said.

I didn't answer. I just put my arm around him.

"I know he used to pick on me all the time, but we were friends. He didn't look too good. I saw them put him in the chopper. Just a glimpse of him. That'll stay with me forever. And that's too long."

Everett came inside.

"We're going now. Smith, stay here with the new guys.

We'll send more men down tomorrow. Guys who know what the fuck they're doing."

Everett looked at me and said, "Let's go, Garrett."

"Hang in there. We'll get through this. Maybe Balsam will send me down here," I told Smith.

"I sure hope so. Be good to have you here."

Smith lowered his head, and I squeezed his shoulder.

Bates drove and Brooks rode up front. Everett and I sat across from one another in the back in the open air. We drove practically to the paved road that led to Song Cau.

Exhaustion and numbness took me out of the present moment. Tainted angels' wings flapped inside my head; connected by a spinner's thread to an angry-loving god; the god who supposedly substitutes love for wrath, while the law of physics and man also offer sacrifices.

I heard that very same law of physics at work; the familiar thud and the distant grumble of the earth. I stared at Everett who cradled his M-79 grenade launcher in his left arm.

"Did you just shoot that?"

He didn't answer.

"Shoot that again, and I'll kill you," I shouted, leveling my weapon from my waist, aiming at Everett's chest. "Do you hear me, you fucking moron?"

The truck sped beyond the trees on my side of the road, over which the corporal's launched grenade had exploded in a small Vietnamese village.

Reaching Song Cau, I lay on my bunk, leaving the universe to swivel on its own axis. At night, suppressing a scream, I bit into bedding, afraid if loosed, I'd lose myself completely; gnashing of teeth, outside the gates of the kingdom, sweating and holding on to an unknown core of me, holding on until daylight.

Tired Gray Soldier

Tired gray soldier

Riding out a breath of tour with me

Deuce-and-a-half

Cargo of two in the rear

North Carolina sergeant face

Burnt from infantry sun

Vacuum eyes terror built

Seeds to suffer from

No fear to see

Not even clean

Had he to cast aside

He wasn't even there I thought

A mold a passer by

The road and dust

Enough to curse

The war inside my heart

Like sinking stones in water wells

Made from trauma shocks

Youth corroded

Life eclipsed

Posterity so chosen

Mannequins of war return

Where youth had left in silence

"There's fire up ahead, Sarge

I see my friend preparing

He's pawing through his ammo vest

To launch grenades

I'm certain

The fire's from the jungle's edge

I see them in the clearing"

The sergeant he didn't move from there

His life inside unwilling

He couldn't bear to win his life

While others had been losing

To see him in that place of his

Scared me more with knowing

That I could be like him

Some time in space some morning

But now it doesn't hurt so much

But maybe in the evening

Before the stars will shine alive

Before my hopes have meaning

Then I'll feel the struggle fierce

My years will keep repeating

It's then I'll know

The soldier gray

Has always been there waiting

* * * *

News spread that Balsam left the platoon, assigned "Special Projects." Everett, promoted to our platoon sergeant, sent Brooks and me near a city, Ben Ket.

I parked the truck and trailer beside a farm road close to a large crater fed by spring water. A tall bare thin tree with only top foliage stood beside the crater and next to the truck, a thick tree provided shade. Wedged between its branches, a multi-colored box, the size and shape of a small open coffin, stood upright. The entire open surrounding area covered about two square miles. Rice paddies separated us visibly two miles from the infantry to the east and less than an eighth-of-a-mile from jungle to the north. Another farm road beside our water point led to two hooches and the jungle. The city lay south out of sight.

While we set up the water point, about ten friendly rural boys ranging in ages from about seven to ten watched all our endeavors. A snake wiggled free from the top of the thin tree and slapped into the water filled crater while bare footed kids surrounded the northern edge. Brooks fired his weapon on automatic.

I ran to him, grabbed him by his shirt and shouted, "Get the hell out of here. I don't care what you do. Stay away from this water point."

"I was shooting at the snake," he said pathetically.

"Those rounds could kill a kid. Don't ever come back here."

His eyes slowly betrayed the joy knowing he'd have no responsibility. He left.

I worked alone every day and made friends with a lot of kids, especially Hue, who was about nine years old, smoked cigarettes and smiled often. His right arm from his shoulder to his hand dangled about as though few bones supported him. Most every day he'd come by smiling to see how things were going, and although I understood little Vietnamese, I understood him.

A month passed during which a huge demand kept me busy days into nights and I slept in different areas of the water point each night. Beneath grass and tarps, I hid soda pop cans, expecting the Cong. My being isolated, alone and exhausted they'd come. Maybe I would hear them.

One afternoon, the cooks, Red and Spiderman walked with Brooks toward the water truck.

"Where you going?" I asked Brooks.

"We have some whores in the bunker."

He pointed west down the road. I knew the barren area; a place Brooks often threw grenades merely to watch them explode.

"Do you have any beer down there?"

"Yes."

"Can I buy a six pack?"

The red head, the alpha dog of the three asked, "What's the matter, you don't like whores?"

"We're all whores in Vietnam," I replied.

"You got a point there," Red agreed. "But everybody need a piece of ass sometime."

"I've taken advantage of them. Not anymore."

I shut down the erdulator and followed them. They began talking ballistics—how an RPG could blow through nine feet of concrete. They kept talking nonsense.

"I'm going back to work the water. I'll buy some beer when you come back if you have any left."

At the water point, the equipment running, I stood at the filter watching the pressure lower. An explosion barely shook the truck. Bombers miles away would occasionally do something similar. I felt a hard slap on my back and I looked behind me thinking a kid slapped me. Nobody there. I looked up and said, "Thanks a lot. I guess the good angels must be looking after me."

I went back to work and a man ran to my position carrying a .45 pistol and a bloodied ammo belt.

"Hurry. Your man is hurt."

"What'd he do shoot himself?"

"No, he got blown up."

He took the .45 out of its holster. Its steel form bent into a half moon.

"Was he wearing that when he got hurt?"

"Yes."

I ran down to the bunker, met by a sergeant who stopped me.

"One of those guys in there works for me."

"You don't need to go in there, son."

They carried Brooks out. His body covered with

slicing and massive wounds. A chopper medevaced him. I watched the chopper ascend; a sacrifice to the god of civilization.

"What happened?" I asked the sergeant.

"An ARVN married to one of the women slammed an RPG round on the ground inside the bunker. Everybody else is dead," the sergeant said.

I went back to the truck, gathered Brooks' belongings and put them outside under a tarp. I felt guilty for running him off the point. Had I been more patient with him he might still be in one piece, but part of me thought he was destined to abandon himself.

The next day a Protestant chaplain gave a memorial service. He seemed like a down-to-earth guy, but I questioned the loving God part, its relation to the war, and the recompense required for the choices the young soldiers had made. Then a Catholic priest served a Mass.

A week later, while I worked the water, a captain and a one-star general appeared. The captain kept yelling at me to stop working and report. The general frowned and calmly quieted the captain.

"Let him finish what he's doing."

The general put his right hand on my shoulder and in a fatherly voice asked me what had happened to Brooks.

I explained.

"Why don't you have a bunker built?" the general asked.

"I don't have time, sir."

"I'll damn sure get one made for you," he said.

Another week passed and Special Projects Balsam showed up, giving orders that made little sense. Heading back to leave by chopper, he announced, "By the way, build a bunker."

A day later a Buddhist priest climbed into the box in the tree next to my truck. He sat there appearing to meditate in his funny robe with his bald head shinning. I jury rigged the sling to my M-16 so that it looped over my shoulder and I could fire it like a pistol with one hand. All day I kept my eye on him while I worked. Maybe he wasn't a priest and maybe he had a weapon under his robe. I got more rattled by the hour, and by the day's end I felt relieved when he finally got out of his box, bowed to me and moved on. Apparently, he too participated in a memorial to the dead, probably for the Vietnamese women and ARVN soldier.

In the days that followed fear rose in me that logic could not deter. The kids no longer came, and I began to think a sniper existed in the jungle's edge with his sights set on me, ready to fire at any moment. Obsessively, the thoughts and then the emotions stifled me, my every movement under deadly scrutiny. No relief came, an endless cycle of thought and fear for days. I kept trying to resist the thoughts and control the fear, but the more I tried the worse I felt. At night, in darkness, I found cover from the fear of a sniper, but the night always brought its own fear.

One day some of the Vietnamese boys finally came to play in the crater of water. Hue climbed high up the thin tree and jumped; his loose arm slapped squarely against the water and he came running to me, crying. I carried him two miles to an infantry medic, a sergeant who spoke Vietnamese. He attended to Hue, still in pain, and told me they'd send him to a hospital and probably cut off his arm. I returned to the water point and the circuit of fear in me receded. A few days later Hue returned, arm still attached, a cigarette in his hand and his eyes smiling.

Still no one came to help me from my platoon.

An afternoon, after working the water inside the erdulator, I saw two infantrymen leading a beautiful Vietnamese girl about eight years old. Her long black shoulder length hair rested on a clean white blouse, and she wore black pants and walked barefooted. Her innocence, her clear fearless eyes not trying to make sense of her captors, looked up at the bigger of the two American monsters. Well over two hundred fifty pounds, an ugly man, his mind and being dedicated to violence, he stopped her, pulled down her black pants and injected her butt with morphine. The other soldier waited and then they moved on in an instant.

Standing on the ground, my weapon in the truck, I gasped, feeling that I had allowed the pedophiles their treachery, while permitting her a lifetime of misery. I feared they'd return to kill me at night; they were infantry and they knew how. I sacrificed her life for mine in a moment of cowardice.

Weariness and guilt beyond belief, I endured, fragmented and tortured, needing to bury my shame.

Finally, the 2nd Battalion sent a recruit to help me work. He pitched a tent next to the crater to sleep and I crawled into the generator trailer, pushed the generator to one side, placed my air mattress down and fell asleep. During the early morning hours, I heard a rocket blast rising high and near our point. I stood to untie the knots of twine but they wouldn't give. The rocket landed about twenty feet from the trailer and didn't explode.

Dark fingers pried; the canvas flap opened. Whites of his eyes widely opened, contrasting with the darkness of night and his skin, the new helper asked, "What was that?"

I heard the thud of a mortar fired from a distant tube.

"I don't know but here comes another one. Get under the truck."

We ran for cover there, but three unknown American soldiers took up most of the space.

"Get with them," I hollered.

Diving for the rear wheels to get my head protected between them, directing my body to wrap around beneath the side of the truck, I scraped the hard road, sliding toward cover. The mortar hit the road about twenty-five feet from me, exploding. All my vision filled with the darkness of night, spaced between bright red jagged shrapnel, bursting hot, with lighter shades of red halos outlining the jagged edges.

The uninvited soldiers, probably an infantry point, ran down the road east. My helper asked if he could run also. I not only agreed I ran with him and we spent the night with the infantry.

A few days later, Everett showed up with his entourage, men from our platoon I barely knew and others from different companies, even his older brother, who followed him around in childlike subservience. Right away, Everett and his men set up tents near the crater and they collected prostitutes for the night of sex, drinking and weed. At about 0200 hours I hadn't slept so I took a shower and changed fatigues. I wore a field jacket over a white towel wrapped around my neck and I looked at the stars as I stood in the road just a ways from the truck when I heard Everett cursing.

"Get out of here you dumb bitch. Didi mau. Sorry stupid whore!"

"What's wrong with you, Everett?" I shouted.

He wouldn't answer, so I kept after him until he answered, "You remember that whore who wore the beret?"

"Yeah."

"It fell off her head, and half her head… and half of her fucking head was missing."

"What do you mean, missing?"

"Just what I said. Her fucking head was missing. It was only half there. It got blown off somewhere."

"Did you look in the tent?"

"Fuck you, Garrett. You're an asshole."

He mumbled something and then poured beer on his genitals. He fiercely rubbed it all over his testicles and penis. His older brother came out of his tent, maybe briefly speculating the purpose of what his little brother was demonstrating, and then he began scrubbing himself with beer too.

Everett and his crew left later in the morning.

Normal work days followed and a scout helicopter

landed in the road. A lieutenant jumped out and said my request for R&R in Hong Kong had been approved. I had forgotten I had submitted it quite some time ago, and I felt amazed Top approved it after our last leave fiasco. The lieutenant said I'd have to catch a ride with anybody going to Song Cau, and that Bates was on his way to replace me.

A convoy came together in a couple days and I rode in the back of a deuce-and-a-half with a staff sergeant. He sat directly behind the cab on the wooden seats facing me, and I sat on the passenger's side of the truck. His face was burnt red from infantry sun and his eyes lost in a solitary wilderness trauma made. He didn't speak, but occasionally glanced at me and smiled oddly. There existed such a total disconnect in him it scared me. If I lived, maybe I'd be something like him.

Half way into the trip, the convoy slowed, and I looked ahead about fifty feet to the next truck in front of us. Michaels, from the Flame Platoon, yanked to remove his vest filled with M-79 rounds.

"Something's happening up ahead," I told the sergeant. "My friend's getting his M-79 ready and I can hear shooting."

The sergeant smiled. He was crazy.

Why is the driver of our truck driving straight into the fight? Can't he stop and let us get off? I could see fifteen to twenty Viet Cong running from a rice paddy toward the jungle. They fired AK-47s at us as they ran. Our truck reached the knoll where rounds zipped past our heads, the highest most observable targets. I grabbed the sergeant to pull him down but he resisted. Rounds ripped the air beside my face and I hit the floor and snaked my way over the side of the truck. I took cover beside a mound of dirt, as a soldier next to me took a round in his thigh. The round slapped him as though one threw a wet wash cloth against a wall. He screamed. Another soldier injected him with morphine. By that time it really had ended, and I watched the soldiers fire volleys into an empty field and into the jungle's edge. I felt something like electricity painfully jolting throughout my insides while I watched the absurd.

A soldier sporting a Mohawk haircut fired wildly with his M-50 mounted to a vehicle. He wheeled about fiercely and shot repeatedly, slicing off the radio antennae attached to his commander's jeep. A sergeant standing in the road open fired with his grease gun, a .45 caliber not capable of reaching the jungle with any accuracy. A cigar jammed in his mouth, he rammed another long clip into his weapon and fired off all the rounds. Then he looked bewildered, as though to question himself: what could he do now or what purpose did he just serve. A weight lifter posing in the road casually fired his M-16 into nothing but the jungle. Only Michaels made any sense. Round after round he fired his grenade launcher over the tree line into the possible route taken by the retreating enemy.

During this fracas I saw a Vietnamese farmer working in the field and I wondered why he didn't seek cover during the attack. I fired a round a couple of feet next to him and the water jumped. He didn't flinch, so I put another round about two feet in front of him and to his side. Again, he didn't respond. As an expert rifleman, I wasn't trying to hit the man; I just couldn't believe he endured the fighting and foolish aftermath without reaction. I wondered how he could accept fate, compared to how I felt with pain coursing throughout my body.

I returned to the truck and the sergeant thanked me

for trying to help him. I swore at him, and he laughed and laughed.

The convoy proceeded to the nearest village next to a tributary, and the Americans chatted excitedly about their exploits. How they had met the challenge, met life head on, how they were heroes, nervous still, and shouting and drinking in an open café.

A day after returning to Sung Cau, I learned that the major from the 7th Brigade had sent a report to the 2nd claiming that I had disrespected him during maneuvers. The person responsible for taking action against me happened to be a warrant officer who disliked me for no apparent reason. He put my name on the infamous levy, and I was given orders to join the infantry.

I packed my gear in a duffle bag, sat on the bare springs of my bunk with the mattress folded up, my weapon and ammo on the floor. Knowing that I'd be headed toward certain death or dismemberment, I waited for someone from the infantry to come after me. Any infantry unit would have stayed away from me in the field because they would have known that I didn't have advanced infantry training, and I could easily set off a trip wire and get someone killed due to my ignorance. My head bowed down, I felt the unforeseen betrayal delivered by another misanthropic officer. The American military, its arrogant misuse of power, was again my enemy. I looked at the floor for some time before I saw the polished boots of Sergeant Monroe Balsam. He took credit for having removed my name from the levy, but that was bullshit; Balsam was only a buck sergeant. Top deserved the credit. But some other man had to take my place, and I'm sure he did not survive just as I would not have.

Goosebumps

Going to Hong Kong, I packed my khaki uniform with the PFC stripes and an extra pair of clean fatigues. Top told Michaels, Hurtado and me that we couldn't carry weapons and we needed to catch a civilian bus to Long Bien. I decided to carry a bayonet knife inside the waistband of my jungle fatigue pants. The three-quarter-length fatigue shirt would conceal it easily. It wasn't much, but still I'd be somewhat armed in Vietnam.

We boarded a Vietnamese bus at midday. Michaels, from the Flame Platoon, and Hurtado, the weight lifter in my platoon, played to the crowd. The village girls giggled and chattered.

Hurtado lit a joint and passed it to Michaels. Grass always made me skittish, but I took a few hits anyway. It didn't help matters when the bus stopped for passengers, and then as it accelerated, a Vietnamese man burst through the rear side doors and skidded across the aisle in front of us. He regained his balance and began jabbering.

"Goddamn GI everywhere I go. I live Chicago five year. You want buy watch?"

He limped heavily and sat down across from me in his civilian clothes. As he pulled out a thin black case filled with Seikos, I saw the grit in him.

"Already got one," Hurtado said.

"What happened to your leg?" Michaels asked.

"I long time soldier. Train your country 1965. Come back my country three year." He pulled up his right pant leg, revealing a nasty scar.

"Must have been tough training," Hurtado said, laughing.

"Shrapnel, I get here my country," he replied, his feelings hurt. He turned to me. "You go Saigon? I know nightclub. It like Chicago."

I didn't answer him.

He remained silent for a long time. Then he went on about the states and how he thought of us as brothers and what it meant to the South Vietnamese, their struggle for freedom, things mostly only a Vietnamese would care about. He turned it all into a bus ride.

We reached Saigon, teeming with its motor scooters and three-wheeler " pizza wagons." We settled for a sleazy motel where prostitutes milled around outside. Hurtado and Michaels said they wanted to rest. It got dark by the time the Vietnamese convinced me to go with him. He said the nightclub was nearby. I didn't want to stay in the motel with the same squalor, and I didn't trust the stranger. But if I could get past this fear, perhaps I'd feel stronger, although I believed this fear surpassed whatever worth I had, or would ever have again.

We walked the poorly lit back streets, overrun with people, mostly men, who moved in and out of the shadows. Sharp and quiet voices mingled with the distant, invisible hum of traffic.

The Vietnamese stopped in front of a run-down two story. "This nightclub. You go upstair. Red door. You open."

"No. You go first."

"No, I need you open."

"If you're screwing with me…"

"It okay. Nightclub."

I stepped into the entryway of the dark, narrow hallway and climbed the stairs. The Vietnamese followed about ten feet behind me. I stopped near the top, and in the dark I could see the red door with a golden knob.

I backed up.

"What wrong? You open door."

I strained to see him more clearly, to study his every movement, to hear every sound, to survive.

He sighed.

Then he climbed the stairs steadily toward me. The knife in my right hand raised, I waited for him to strike first. I'd give him that much. His leg buckled and his body fell against me, and I stabbed him on the left side of his neck near his throat. He tumbled down the stairs and lay sprawled out on the sidewalk. I couldn't see his head, just his chest down to his feet.

I sat down near the top stairs and looked at his lifeless body. I sat there for what seemed like a long time, but I wasn't sure, and I didn't think or feel anything. No remorse, no fear, nothing, just a familiar numbness but more like a paralysis. Then I saw his body moving out of my sight. His shoes were the last things I saw moving. The war dragged him away.

I put the knife inside my waist band and rolled up my fatigue shirt sleeves. Cupping my hands under my chin, elbows on my knees, some part of me joined the empty space on the sidewalk. I heard the red door open, the loud music blaring and the distinct voice of a maître-d' casually inviting me inside.

A thriving nightclub scene flooded my vision. I saw a large blonde American woman in a black cocktail dress singing from a small stage. Musicians played. A bevy of bald American men in tuxedos with younger Western women sat at tables covered with white linen.

A waiter led me to a darkened, obscure corner, but not far enough away for me to misperceive the laughter and safe chatter of the affluent; the people somehow profiting from the war, responsible for it, and for me in it.

Eventually the nightclub began to drown me and I thought about Abraham preparing to sacrifice Isaac. What the hell did that mean? I began to get sick of the people around me. Anger turned into nausea and nausea turned into nonbeing.

I left and went outside into the streets where the universe made sense again, where I belonged in the war and it belonged in me; it always had and it always would. I sensed that if feelings surfaced they would crush me, so I avoided looking for any body of evidence that would further condemn me.

In my room I washed the knife blade and remembered stabbing a short fat snake and seeing Hue stiffen his body, mimicking rigor mortis. I smiled, thinking he probably thought I was brave when really I was only pissed off. I washed myself, changed fatigues and lay on the bed in the dark until daylight.

I wrote a note for Michaels telling him I had changed my mind and didn't want to go to Hong Kong. Said I was going back to Song Cau. I pinned the note to his shirt while he slept, and caught a ride with a convoy.

In Song Cau, Top looked puzzled when he saw me and he asked, "What the hell's the matter with you, Garrett? I give you a break and you don't take it."

"You've given me plenty of breaks, Top, and I'm grateful."

"You're a strange kid."

"I'd rather not leave the war and have to come back to it."

"I see," he said, and went back to his paperwork.

"Hong Kong, Vietnam, it's all the same, so what's the point?"

He looked up at me. "I'm leaving soon, and the new first sergeant goes by the book, so keep your nose clean. You'll be all right. Now go find something to do. You're beginning to annoy me."

I pulled normal duty for several days until, one evening, Sergeant Balsam told me we were going to take filter parts to Khong Dan early the next morning.

Earlier in the morning than expected, we entered the motor pool and I began the usual inspection of the deuce-and-a-half. Balsam wrung his hands repeatedly and frowned. The yard was empty. Most of the soldiers were either getting showered or dressed or moving toward the mess hall.

I leaned over the open hood of the platoon's deuce-and-a-half to check the water level in the radiator. I replaced the cap, squeezed the top hose and checked the belts to see if they were frayed. I looked at Balsam and reckoned the depth of his irritability. "What's the big rush?" I asked before I crawled beneath the truck.

"You should of done that last night. I told you I wanted to leave early. Never mind looking at everything. Get up here."

I pulled myself up by the bumper and wiped my hands on a dirty rag. "You never go anywhere, so what's the big deal about Khong Dan?"

"We need to leave here before Top come around and make me stay here all day," he said, and then looked annoyed for having explained himself.

"Believe me you can pick a better joy ride than this."

"This ain't no joy ride. We got to deliver parts down there. Smith broke down and the infantry crying about it."

I looked at Balsam's clean fatigues and the spit shined leather portion of his jungle boots. His flak vest and the camouflage cloth covering his helmet had been scrubbed spotless and there was absolutely nothing written on it. Every soldier wrote something on his helmet cloth: Leroy, Betty, Boogeyman, something, but not Balsam. He was dressed for the war but not really in it.

"Okay Sarge, get in."

We drove out of the motor pool, down the road beside the S-4 yard, with its stacks of pallets filled with military parts, past the Battalion Headquarters and then beyond the chapel. We passed the massage parlor and laundry near the entrance to Song Col and then headed down the road toward Chung Quyen.

Balsam had not spoken a word.

"You want to stop somewhere and get a milkshake?" I finally asked.

"What the fuck's the matter with you? There ain't no milkshake in this bitch."

"You sure about that?"

"Shut up, Garrett," he said, and half-grinned for an instant before he returned to his brooding.

We drove along the paved streets of Chung Quyen until we reached the entrance to the Khong Dan road. Along the northern side of the road, a wire fence stretched nearly a hundred yards. About thirty Vietnamese farm workers squatted along the fence line, waiting to work the rice. I pulled the truck slowly onto the dirt road and stopped about fifty feet in.

"What are you stopping for?" Balsam asked.

"I don't know. Something doesn't feel right."

"Well don't be stopping here. Get down the road."

"Something's wrong," I said distantly.

Suddenly, a Vietnamese man jumped onto the running board next to my open window, startling me. The friendly worker smiled, displaying large crooked teeth. He pointed in the direction down the road, speaking only Vietnamese but gesturing excitedly.

I understood. Fear rose inside my stomach.

Balsam squirmed. He stared over his shoulder in the direction of the Vietnamese workers and I heard the strain in his voice as he spoke. "What are you waiting for? I told you to go."

I nodded toward the Vietnamese sitting along the fence line and said, "You're afraid of them. Aren't you?"

"I ain't afraid of nobody," he said and then he looked away from me.

"They just work the rice," I said, "Look at them, they don't have any guns. You got a machine gun for Christ's sake."

"I don't care who they are, we need to get down there," he said.

"We can't go down the road until they sweep the mines. It's not eight o'clock yet."

"There ain't no mines in the road, and I'm ordering you to drive."

"You don't understand. They sweep the road every day at eight o'clock. We're too early."

"How do you know that?"

"I just know it, and this guy reminded me."

"You don't understand no Vietnamese. How do you know what he's saying?"

"He's pointing down the road and his voice is excited. He's saying something I already know, but I've never been here this early before."

"No way," Balsam said, and he looked away disgustedly.

"They're not screwing around. They'll blow our legs off."

Balsam didn't answer.

I could hear the Vietnamese man breathing.

"An APC hit a mine on this road not too long ago and it blew everybody up. I'm telling you the truth."

"That ain't true. You'd remember that before now. But you're here, and we got to get down there. This the last time I'm going to tell you, Garrett. This an order!"

Angrily, I told the Vietnamese to get off the truck. He stepped off the running board and once more pointed down the road, but this time with less enthusiasm.

I drove the truck forward and looked over the hood at the narrow road passing. Shortly into it I prayed the "Our Father" to myself. Then I started talking to God in my thoughts.

"Now what the hell am I supposed to do? What am I supposed to do?"

"*You got to calm down first or you won't know what to do,*" I heard the voice in my thoughts say. So I quieted down and listened.

"*What do you know about this road?*"

"Well, I know everybody knows it's mined except for Balsam."

"*So what does that tell you?*"

That he's a stupid fucker."

"*No, I mean about the road. What does that tell you about the road, that everybody knows it's mined? Who are they trying to kill if everybody knows it's mined?*"

I paused.

"They're trying to kill the people who don't know it's mined," I thought.

"*That's right. And where would they drive?*"

"Right down the tracks."

"*Okay, so stay off the tracks as much as you can and drive into the mud holes, right into the deep water. They won't bury a mine in the deep mud. They'll put them on the road. And look for marks where they have been tampering with the dirt and drive completely off the road whenever you can.*"

I leaned into the steering wheel and began to drive.

Mud holes formed here and there in varying lengths and depths. They were separated from one another by stretches of dry road. I stayed off the road to one side. Then I had to cross the tracks for the first time and I felt the chill of it. The road veered north.

The deuce-and-a-half troop carrier rattled in the rear.
The seats along both sides of the bed made of wooden
slats connected with metal hinges shook every time
I drove into a mud hole and out. The truck lurched
and bounced and sometimes slid. The suspension
hammered into the frame every time I drove into a
hole and it sounded like the beginning of explosions.
My body jolted, and I gripped the wheel more tightly,
my face inches away from the windshield.

Balsam shouted, "Drive the truck in the road, and stay
out of the holes."

I could hear myself shouting back, "I'm driving this
truck, and you don't even know what's going on, so
shut the fuck up!"

Balsam didn't answer; he just stared passively out the
passenger's window at the rice fields.

We drove past a farmer's cottage, and suddenly I
remembered the last time I had passed there with
a stoned soldier in the back of a three-quarter. I
remembered him putting his weapon on automatic
and shooting into large flocks of geese in the field next

to the cottage. Blood and white bodies. Squawking. Wings flapping. Feathers. He had shot them for no reason and I remember feeling lost inside, like there was nothing I could do about it.

"That farmer put mines in the road; there's no doubt about it," I thought. "This is how you die. I should have sandbagged the floor. I should have refused to drive down here. I should have gone back to Chung Quyen and waited for the sweeps."

I glanced at Balsam who seemed to be enjoying himself. A breeze blew across his big face, and he half closed his eyes. I shook my head in disbelief.

Mostly dry ground spread for about a couple hundred feet beyond the empty geese field. I strained to see marks in the road where the farmer might have buried a mine and I drove off the road as soon as possible.

Somehow, I could feel myself outside of my body, like next to me, not above looking down, just next to me. It felt as though my eyes kept the weight of my entire body suspended, that I could stay outside of myself somehow because my eyes kept me from collapsing.

My hands gripped the steering wheel, but I couldn't

feel them. I couldn't feel the rest of my body except in flashes, and then my mind became like a spirit, disconnected, light and feathery, floating, somehow hurting, but not feeling it, and then feeling it like the white geese being blown apart and flopping around in slow motion. Their spastic twitching bodies with holes forming. Dark red dots. Blood spreading over whiteness. Squawking. Orange beaks. Little eyes. Movement and pain.

Goose bumps.

I felt goose bumps along my arms and legs. The thin blond hair on my forearms bent at the tips. It were as though they floated into the motion of the road passing beneath the wheels. A cold chill covered my neck. It moved into my throat and stayed. I felt the sweat behind my knees. The sweat of my shirt sticking to my back. The weight of my flak-vest. My scalp tight beneath my helmet. My body floating.

I drove like this for about an hour and then I recognized the jungle where it jutted out into the rice paddies too close to the road on Balsam's side. I knew Khong Dan was near. The road dried out and then I saw in the distance the guard shack at the entrance to the firebase. I felt the tension recede, but it stayed in me somehow, attached to an unrecognizable space, still floating but hurting like nothing I had ever felt. I remembered my father telling me not to take anything for granted. Immediately, I drove off the dry road to one side and continued, until finally, an MP waved me inside the compound.

I drove the truck into the yard in front of the watermen's hooch. I got out of the truck and as I stood on the ground I felt as though I were suspended by my head, like a clothespin on a wire, but I couldn't feel my head. My awareness had no center, yet I could feel my legs moving toward the shack. Removing my helmet, I ran my fingers through my hair while I walked. I sighed and then I wondered why I couldn't feel the energy of the sigh inside me.

Balsam seemed to be talking to Smith who stood in the doorway, his eyes fixed on me. Balsam then walked away and I could barely hear his voice; something about he'd be back soon.

"What the hell's wrong with you?" Smith asked me.

"We just drove down here and they hadn't swept the road yet. Balsam wouldn't listen."

"Come inside," Smith said, and he led me into the hooch like he was helping an old man.

Inside, a fan resting on a chair blew air in the direction of his bunk in the far corner. The only light that filtered into the room came through a few cracks in the wall. The distinct music of Jimmy Hendrix blasted from a reel-to-reel tape recorder. Smith lowered the volume.

"Lie down on my bunk."

"Oh, I don't need to do that."

"Just lie down."

He took my helmet and rifle and put them on the table. I pulled off my flak vest and listlessly slung it over a chair. I lied on the bunk on my back and closed my eyes. In the middle of the room he toiled to open a round plastic bottle.

He cursed.

I smiled faintly.

Finally, he pried the lid off and popped two small white pills into his hand. He poured water into his canteen cup.

"Take these."

"What are they?"

"French tranquilizers. Just take them."

I swallowed one and lay down again and drifted off.

About twenty minutes later, Balsam returned and wanted me to drive the truck back to Chung Quyen immediately. I refused. I said I wouldn't go anywhere until the road had been swept.

We argued for what seemed like a long time.

Another sergeant from the Khong Dan firebase came into the hooch and said the mine sweep had formed and we could line up in a convoy. Balsam left the hooch and rode with somebody else. I drove the same truck back alone. Where I had remembered my father telling me not to take anything for granted, the demolition team detonated one mine. Near the empty field of geese, they set off a larger one. It was a plate mine, the kind that bores its way through a vehicle and then explodes in the open space. When they detonated it, the soil spewed into the air over fifty feet in a tight stream, like water from a fireman's hose, then the dirt spread out and fell to the muddy ground.

It seemed like rain falling. I listened and watched it splatter.

Daylight Again

Athree-week storm in California delayed my exit from Vietnam and I caught up with Smith. He and I and a large group of veterans stood in the Tan Son Nhut hangar, waiting for our replacements to arrive. When they did, we headed quietly toward the jet, where the passing of tours happened with hardly a sound or hint of emotion.

We flew to San Francisco where inside the airport a huge plate glass separated the veterans from the public who were busy eating in a restaurant, gawking at us. How they looked at us without acknowledging where we came from and what we had endured. They looked so bored and unaware that food stuck to some of their older faces.

Smith's parents met us after having driven from Parma, Idaho. His father seemed to be an older but exact version of Smith and his mother looked like a large Norman Rockwell mother archetype. Embraces all around.

"You've got my phone number and address," I said. "We'll always stay in touch. You're the brother I never had."

Smith cried. My eyes misted.

We hugged and they left.

I called my brother, Ryan, who lived in San Francisco.

"We're pickin' and a grinnin'," he said. "Keep your shirt on. There's no VC down there is there? We'll come get you after a while."

I knew I didn't want to see him. Let him look for the VC. Let him look forever so he could say he went to Vietnam too. I took a flight to Chicago, stayed in a hotel room drinking bourbon and water. In the following afternoon, I flew to Boston.

Before boarding a bus to Vermont, I saw a hippie hearse plastered with peace signs and flower stickers. In big bold multi-colored letters painted on the back, it read: Good for One Ride.

A few hours later that night, I asked the bus driver to let me off by a bridge in Cold River, Vermont. I stood on the bridge momentarily and watched the river flow and then I walked past the sawmill, up a small hill, across the railroad tracks and then climbed the steep dirt road bordered by forest on both sides. Another bridge, small and wooden, built disproportionately to the curve in the road, led abruptly to the last ascent.

The sky lit with moon and stars, the meadows tamped and weathered brown, no sight of snow, I could see the maple orchard clearly in the distance. I finally reached the house and heard the wind strike the metal pulley against the metal flag pole.

The key still lodged in the rotted eve above the stone covered well, I unlocked the door to the summer kitchen and then entered the kitchen. The empty house seemed smaller than ever. I walked in the dark to the sink and drank water and then to the stairs leading to the open chamber. I opened the door to the finished room with the gray pitched walls and the tall gun cabinet supporting a television plugged into the naked ceiling fixture. Twisting the light bulb on, I sat down on the sagging relic of a bed, undressed, twisted the light bulb off, and lay awake beneath the buffalo-robe bedspread until daylight.

Author's Note

Harsh and surreal events led to my getting drafted into the war, and that descent began after my first year of junior college basketball. I remember tasting blood the night of 19 May 1966, and seeing the car lights from the highway appear and disappear against the distant forest background thinking I need to move near the highway so someone could see me. After driving eighteen hundred miles nonstop from the Southwest, I had fallen asleep. The car flew over a fifteen foot bank and smashed into huge boulders, crushing the left side of me and the complete driver's side of the vehicle. It landed in a small pasture which descended about forty-five degrees and was dissected by a brook that cut into the field at least ten feet, forming a narrow gully. I knew I was damaged internally, but in my confusion I headed toward the lights against the tree line and I stumbled over rocks and fell into a brook, bordered by thin brush in the Vermont cow pasture.

I lay unconscious for some time, until in flashes of brief single flickers, I saw my body being lifted manually out of the gully and onto a gurney. Later, I experienced another flash of urban lights outside

the hospital entrance and then I blacked out. Inside
the emergency room, I remembered being awake for
a moment and knowing they were cutting through
my favorite green corduroy pants and pullover shirt,
and how that seemed to bother me. Three days later
I awoke from a coma in the ICU. I saw through the
open doorway my cousin Dawna, standing in the
hallway with her hands cupped over her mouth and
her body shifting to one side and back again. I could
barely wave to her before she left crying.

I soon learned that most of my ribs were broken
and that one or two had pierced and collapsed my
left lung. My fourth and fifth lumbar vertebrae were
broken and my left wrist had been sliced down to the
nerve, completely numbing my hand.

After one week, they wheeled me down into the
basement, helped me onto a table and turned on
several harsh overhead lights. Momentarily, I saw
within the beams of light dust particles spinning
in the air and floating. No one gave me anesthesia
because the doctor feared the operation might collapse
my other lung. He lowered from the ceiling a huge
metal apparatus that housed an electric drill, which
he guided roughly three inches down and to the right

from my broken left collar bone stopping the bit just above my chest. He told me the procedure would hurt and he gave me a rubber mouth piece to bite. He squeezed the trigger and the bit whistled while he lowered the drill. I saw the sequence for a moment until a nurse pulled my head back to the right. She had a stern matronly look on her face, but it didn't matter because I could see the drill's reflection in her glasses. When it bored through my chest cavity, the trapped air sizzled out. With my broken ribs, I could hardly inhale in the first place, but when the pain hit me, I took in several deep breaths, each of which expanded my broken ribs and hurt more than the actual drill's penetration. My body flailed about and I cursed. I could not catch my breath and every time I inhaled deeply, it hurt. I could not calm down. I did finally recover and the doctor lectured me about cursing and my emotional immaturity, but I didn't care and he didn't care either but the nurse with the big white face and glasses scowled.

They hauled me back to my room and shoved a tube through the hole in my chest. They drained a gallon of dead blood out of me during the next three weeks, during which I moaned more often than I didn't, and the nurses eagerly gave me morphine. When things finally settled, I read James Bond novels during the day and screamed at night. My mother claimed it was because of the novels: the villains, the violence and the magical killing nonsense, but the undertone in her delivery clearly discouraged screaming. But, I *was* screaming.

That first night, Dr. Tomasi told my mother that I had a fifty-fifty chance of survival because I was in tremendous physical shape before the accident. He didn't know that I had just finished playing one year of junior college basketball three hours a night without relief on the scrub team—the five of us— against a deluded coach and his eight man rotation. We ran about ten miles a night against bigger, better and stronger players—most were Black athletes from Chicago—four would eventually play Division One and "Hands," the small forward, would later become a Globetrotter.

Just before I left the hospital weighing one hundred and twenty pounds, the wind blew through the hospital corridor and I tried to close the door to my room, but I didn't have enough strength. Shortly afterwards, I went home with a cast on my left arm.

Within a month I tore off the cast and I began lifting small weights on the wooden floor of the hayloft in our empty cow barn.

In the fall I returned to college and continued to work out alone with weights. By January 1967, the coach allowed me back on the basketball team and I regained my scholarship, but he ridiculed me while I shuffled down the court like an old man, spitting blood on the sidelines. He wanted to see me humiliated, but by March I ran fast breaks against his team and in one practice, he put Hands on my side with three walk-ons to run against his four starters and the sixth man. We ran them off the court and Hands praised me, "You can play with anyone!" In a later practice the coach announced, "McGinnis only plays when *he* wants to."

We were beaten in the first round of the junior college playoffs.

I left college in March, and the notion that I would be drafted after leaving the deferral college allowed had suddenly become a massive life threatening intrusion when I received my draft notice. There existed a strong self-sabotaging element in my decision to leave college when Johnson and America's corporate sponsored war began gearing up, but that's when the "what's-the-use" part of me surfaced. I knew I didn't have the money to continue my education without an athletic scholarship and I knew the coach would have never helped me to get on with a small four-year college basketball team.

Reading the draft notice, I plummeted into an existential emptiness and dread difficult to describe. In the following weeks had I focused on the injuries I had sustained the year before, and pursued that tract toward draft deferment, the outcome probably would have been different. But I had believed that my basketball training and my resilience were reasons enough for my draft eligibility. My beliefs regarding my recovery from the car accident were immersed in a childlike ego state, and my actions to thwart the negative emotional momentum were ineffective. I thought I wouldn't fail an Army physical even though I had no feeling in my left hand and the nerve had bunched into a ball under the flesh at my wrist. I had always overlooked my serious injuries in the way youth think they are immortal, until the years accumulate and their strength diminishes

Seized by the United States to become a government-issued soldier, I had been served with the decision either go to war or go to prison. Montreal, only two hundred miles from my hometown, might as well have been a cave in the Pacific Ocean as far as I was concerned. I was a Vermonter after all, and supposedly a Yankee steeped in the fighting tradition of the Green Mountain Boys—men who had been heralded in the American Revolution and the Civil War, WWII and Korea. I had been raised by parents whose ancestors were Kelts, the Indo-European highland warriors who had attacked the lowlanders with picks and axes, the likes of which inspired Mel Gibson's Braveheart. And my father often played bagpipes while dressed in his kilt and Scottish plaids and Glengarry. He repeatedly told stories how he had fought an older classmate named Arthur Bartlett, how he had throttled the piss out of him in the tall grass while his twin brother (the weaker one) held his books. But in spite of all that hoopla my heritage and culture and family had produced, my mind became filled with the fear of oblivion and it stretched beyond cartoon proportions.

After a week of driving the back roads in Vermont, I

realized that I had some choices left to avoid the draft, so I tested with the Coast Guard and the recruiter liked my results. No other branches of service were available, but I reasoned that the Coast Guard would be the safest choice remaining and the least likely to be involved in the war. But, eventually my medical history became a problem, and the recruiter said I needed to get the surgeon's clearance in writing before they would accept me. I was so nervous and disassociated, that in my excitement, when I went to the physician's home on a weekend to get his input, I misunderstood him. He said, "Is this what you really want to do?" And I said yes, I want to join the Coast Guard, but what he really meant was did I want to join any military branch after having experienced such severe injuries. I didn't understand or respond to the moment, instead I reacted in fear, and all I could think about was getting thrown into the infantry and getting my legs blown off or getting captured or tortured or killed. So, Yes! I want to join.

He signed a statement indicating that I was fit for the Coast Guard. Later, I gave the statement to the recruiter and in a few days he came to my home and told me the Coast Guard denied my application because they feared complications might surface from my damaged lung. Then he said he gave all of my paperwork, including the medical clearance Dr. Tomasi had signed, to the Army. I couldn't believe he had done that; he had just kicked me in the testicles, and it became obvious that I was destined to go to war and there was nothing I could do about it. There wasn't anything like an intermediate solution; if I went into the Army, I was going to Vietnam.

Finally, I went to Manchester, New Hampshire in a bus to take an Army physical, where a little old man, a Specialist 6, a nurse or something, read my paperwork and he took me by the arm and said, "You don't have to go." "I don't have to go!" I said in a loud voice, and he shook his head "no, you don't have to go." A captain in a nearby office heard my voice, and he said, "Bring that man in here." I went into his office and he read Dr. Tomasi's report, and then he said to me "There's nothing wrong with you." And to the little old man he said, "Process him."

✶ ✶ ✶ ✶

Good for One Ride describes the 1968 Tet Offensive experienced by a combat engineer water purification specialist. The first person point of view chronicles the gradual psychological fragmentation of self endured by the protagonist, Theo Garrett. The work provides insight into the thoughts and feelings of a soldier whose perception of the war is drawn from mid-level combat exposure, and depicts several warfare traumas without emphasizing the usual gore that often brutalizes the reader. The novel provides interactions between the American combatants who exist in contrasting life styles. There is a balance between narrative and dialogue, sprinkled with humor in this fast-paced work, written intentionally in a direct but sometimes lyrical manner that provides action accompanied by soldiers' feelings and thoughts, as they face a constant existential surrealism teetering between their longing for survival and their fear of oblivion.

Not intending to dispel the reincarnation theory, I have often thought of my life in terms of good for one ride—irony and sarcasm included. There is nothing good about war. Since I am aware that my life and the lives of my Vietnam veteran friends have been severely affected by trauma, I thought the title would provide the reader a sense that war continues without mercy in the minds and spirits of the combat veterans who do return. I thought of the title in 1989 after receiving a two months' supply of bus tokens to go to and from a Veterans Administration's outpatient post-traumatic-stress-disorder program. Instead of the inscription "good for one ride" the bus tokens read "one adult fare." Most of the young soldiers, myself included, who were drafted into the war were emotionally undeveloped and basically we were children headed for a death ride in an American foreign policy circus.

I intended to show the insanity and surrealism of the Vietnam War by what the protagonist Theo Garrett endured during his mid-level combat tour. The protagonist's traumatic experience and his thoughts and reactions to those traumas provided a clear message that war dehumanizes man, and depicted how a person gets post-traumatic-stress-disorder. The work showed how suffering from terror possessed the protagonist and rendered him unable to determine reality. Conveying his thoughts and emotions risked sounding melodramatic, so I handled that carefully. Merely reporting events could have easily turned the characters into caricatures, and I definitely wanted to avoid that stigma. American soldiers are human beings whose psychological and biological natures are not meant to withstand the constant onslaught of terror and the threat of death.

Some threats faced by my protagonist originate from unlikely sources. At a young age, he needs to be able to evaluate the intelligence and combat experience of his superiors. Some of their decisions will thrust him into unnecessary combat; his awareness may not be enough to alleviate the threats, but it demands he trust his instincts. In one particular incident, he is ordered by an inexperienced sergeant to drive through a mined road that he would have avoided had he been alone. In another situation, he is under attack in a small American firebase located near a city. The frontal assault takes place on the farthest side of the base away from his position. When the action subsides, there are twenty or more American GIs–including officers–standing and facing the city, completely exposed by the light of flares. Garrett stays in a bunker "feeling" something is wrong, but his best friend in the war badgers him into coming out into the light. There again, he does not trust his instincts. His training has taught him to seek cover, but under social pressure he concedes, and he is immediately faced with a sniper's round. From *Good for One Ride*, the following is the protagonist's reaction to the sniper's shot:

"God and war were at opposite poles like pleasure and torture, like prostitutes and the Virgin Mary. Now, they have become one. It happened with a flash of light that I saw. A sniper's round missed my face and dug into the bunker wall. I felt dread tear my heart with cold scissors. Will it ever mend this unapparent wound? Perhaps it keeps tearing as I go along. Finally, the heart falls from its place and takes a turn down inside my right leg or my left. The skin at the anklebone is strung so tightly there. The blood bursts forth. It fills my boot and sloshes around with every step. I hear it in my sleep and there is no resting place."

In another trauma, he hears a rocket launched directly upon his position and instead of staying down, he stands up in terror, seeking another place for cover, as the missile lands not far from him. A few months into the war, huge emotional pressure attacks Garrett's nervous system and it provokes further his illogical decisions. At some point, training and experience aren't enough to defuse his reaction to terror, and from that space I emphasize how terror, the fear of future terror, sleep deprivation and the experiencing of many surrealistic traumatic events deconstruct my protagonist's self. There is a tipping-point in this survival test when Garrett reaches the space where he can no longer try to survive. He's like an old man who can't fight and can't run; he can only continue numb and so devoid of strength that he is unable to see the war. In response to this challenge, his training and his will to live need to kick in. At this crossroad, survival in warfare depends on what is left of his will, the grace given to him and his hope that grace exists.

Dealing with the after effects from the war required a strong will to survive, and this statement is unfortunately supported by the fact that many Vietnam veterans have committed suicide since the war. To some extent, the American culture restricted me from seeking medical help until I consistently could no longer operate in a work environment without incident. Americans see themselves as strong and independent and able to endure suffering without help, especially help that is psychiatric in nature. The mental, physical and emotional pain emanating from nightmares, flashbacks, hyper-vigilance, anxiety attacks, suicidal ideation and the huge loss of sleep— to name a few side effects—forced me in 1984 to seek a psychologist outside of the Veterans Administration (VA). I took a Minnesota Multi-phasic Personality Inventory Test and scored negatively off the charts in every component. The psychologist sent me to a psychiatrist who misdiagnosed me as manic depressive and prescribed Lithium and Elavil, the effects of which increased my weight from 170 pounds to 230 pounds.

In 1989, I endured a VA post-traumatic-stress program where the head of the program, a counseling psychologist "flooded" me. Just prior to the flooding, I wrote a narrative describing a trauma, after which the psychologist took me into a small room, applied bio-feedback tabs to the outside of my head and chest, and then slowly recounted the trauma audibly until either some of the grief and terror energy trapped inside me got released or became further impacted. In my case, trapped energy pumped out of my mouth in nine chugs which I heard inside me like an air compressor recharging. I continued to work full-time a couple years later, and in 1995 I suffered heart pain which drove me into therapy, fortunately with a competent Ph.D. therapist contracted by the VA.

The first two years of that therapy threw me into

terror night and day. I had quit Lithium and Elavil by myself, and the VA put me on benzodiazepine tranquilizers and hypnotics to help me sleep. But after taking four tranquilizers and two 10-milligram pills of Zolpidem each night, I would awake within an hour or so, completely dominated by terror and unable to fall sleep again. Also, during that period of time, I suffered from colitis. It's amazing how much endurance I needed to survive that onslaught, and the amount of self-awareness I needed to protect myself further from countless psychiatrists and their prescriptions, to include the likes of Haldol, Thorazine, Remeron, and Loxapine. I calibrated each medication and never took the full amount prescribed until I knew precisely how I would react to the lower doses. The real therapy lasted for over 10 years, and it gave me clear insight regarding the reenactments often triggered. Anyone facing similar combat reactions would benefit from working in counseling therapy, but one should expect a few trials before finding a real effective professional therapist.

My perception of the war involves survival responses faced by a mid-level combat survivor. In other words, I did not pursue the enemy like infantrymen, but dealt with the war that pursued me. I've mentioned that a soldier at this level needs to trust his instincts and never take anything for granted. I would watch everything and everybody connected to the Vietnamese. There was no telling who was who, and no exact determination ever existed. When I worked alone two miles from the infantry, I feared the enemy would sneak up on me while I slept, so I put soda pop cans under tarps and under grass that I had spread around my point, and I slept in different places every night. I made friends with Vietnamese children who often supplied me with more information than Army intelligence. Granted, Army intelligence never communicated with me, so I took the matter into my own hands.

The kids would come to me after an attack on my position and they would tell me, "VC come tonight, you stay at my house." So, I'd pack up my weapon and rounds and head over to see the family, and depending on where they existed, they might have risked retaliation from the enemy. During attacks on small firebases, I handled the situations apart from the other American combatants connected to other units, and I was often alone. I did not expect any different scenario and I understood this GI sociology. It was imperative that I clean my weapon often. Too many soldiers faced the enemy with rounds jammed inside their weapons. I've mentioned that officers sometimes made judgments that were not sound, and there existed an element of revenge in their decisions. This also applied to sergeants, who for one reason or another sent me to field positions where I was accompanied by the weakest and most unstable platoon member.

Survival depended upon recognizing and sizing up anyone sent to accompany me. I had to run people off my point whom I had seen frozen during other attacks. I mean they were unable to respond and they became dangerous to those of us preparing. Oddly enough, sometimes, if I were facing attack, a platoon sergeant who resented me would actually look for me to side with him, and I looked for him as well. It paid dividends to make friends with my superiors, especially the First Sergeant, and to avoid conversation or interaction with officers who could expose me to traumatic situations. There is nothing glamorous about war, and the only time I thought I showed courage was when I responded to an attack while others stayed inside bunkers. But shortly after that, another incident would occur and I would have a cowardly reaction. Survival depended on my flexibility to erase self-condemnation and to continue facing the unknown.

* * * *

After my tour in Vietnam, I reentered civilization by helping build the valleys of a waste water treatment plant in Vermont. Fueled by my youthful power, I out-worked everyone, man-handling the hours, shoveling the earth without pause, leveling uneven ground, tamping steep banks, running with Georgia buggies filled with mortar and finishing the work late into the evenings. The nights turned into early morning hours, part of which I shot solitary pool at the local American Legion. Loyal patrons sat on nearby bar stools, males and females in their forties and fifties, often times shouting with joy for no apparent reason. When they managed to quiet themselves, I could hear only the sound of the pool balls clacking in domino effect. It was then that I recognized the patron's emptiness, but I didn't care that their grief-filled lives mirrored mine.

Saturdays, the host who tended the bar most times wore one of those pointed hats with badges and medals but he always showed me kindness and he made Yankee beef stew filled with plenty of meat and vegetables. I had only to buy one bowl and thereafter, like a Buddhist with outstretched hand and bowl, I poured countless scoops from a huge metal pot into my bowl for the rest of the day, and I drank beer for which I paid. I drank and kept shooting solitary pool until every so often, only on Saturdays, the Colonel showed up around 7:00 p.m. to compete. He came with his own cue stick, the kind you unscrew and carry in a case, and he brought his wife and daughter, and I always beat him at nine-ball. I never knew if he really had been a colonel, but otherwise why would he have such a nickname? His daughter liked me and after several weekends she said she wanted to cook for me at her place, but I was too restless for Vermont and too wired for anything manipulative.

The more righteous hometown folk outside the daytime legion depressed me, and I felt that they had capitulated in drafting me into the war. When they saw me on the streets they avoided me, as though the war was my war and mine alone, and how I dealt with the unspoken dehumanization and trauma was my business. I was supposed to somehow miraculously transform anew, sparkling alive back into their dull society without pause, as though nothing had happened to me, and I was to allow everyone to believe and act as though we were all innocent and we were supposed to forget about everything. We were Americans after all. And we still had GIs in Vietnam and, of course, there was a reason and a moral decency in support of the war. The government had declared it so, even though Daniel Ellsberg's efforts later proved otherwise, but something about allowing that untruth and belief in our country's righteousness blinded the civilians, or left them numb, but not numb like me.

I consciously carried that lie just like everyone else in my hometown, but I carried it with an abscess in my unconscious and it would spread into a cancer that I could not feel. Submerged beneath my flat affect, it would continue the work of guerrilla warfare, sifting me and fragmenting every cell of whatever self remained in me. It lived and operated in the struggle to challenge my every decision, which it cleaved in half and half again and more...

Made in the USA
San Bernardino, CA
23 January 2018